TOFU INK ARTS PRESS

VOLUME 6

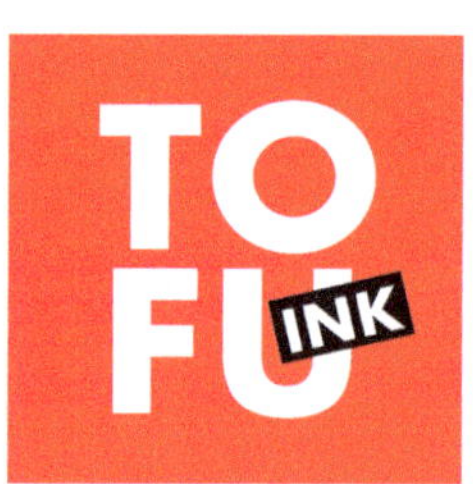

Tofu Ink Arts Press Volume 6

Published by Tofu Ink Arts Press. All rights reserved.
Book design by JLTY Atelier
Cover image courtesy of Abol Bahadori

ISBN: 978-1-958661-12-3

www.TOFUINK.com
A member of CLMP

Dedicated to

My Husband Michael Thye Peng Ngo

"To consecrate the union between elsewhere and possibility,
the poet demanded of himself permanent abstinence
from something impossible."

- Poetics of Relation, Edouard Glissant

CONTENTS

PREFACE

"A concept is a brick. It can be used to build a courthouse of reason. Or it can be thrown through the window."

"Bring something incomprehensible into the world!"

"Writing has nothing to do with meaning. It has to do with landsurveying and cartography, including the mapping of countries yet to come."

— Gilles Deleuze

Tofu Ink Arts Press absorbs in possibilities; the possibilities our poets and artists share with our readers in our *Volume 6* edition. The reader IS the writer, and we invite you to imagine! Our writers and artists rupture, mapping at times a-linearly & all proliferating, without boundaries or centers, in the margins without limits, rejecting principles of hegemony, creating a desire, that is always in flux, along new pathways of experimentation. Tofu Ink contributors manifest possibility; a sort of, what I like to call a ***Rhizomatic Poetic.*** This poetic inquiry explores diverse artistic acts; poetic discursive narratives, mutating through exploring memory, decolonizing, otherness, romanticization of the other and subsequently sometimes with elicit performances of queer identity, with overlapping Rhizomatic voices in errantry.   These artists are the true auditors of our world, for discovering every possible elsewhere; a liberating vehicle into possibilities. The arts may be the only medium to weave these difficult tasks.

Tofu Ink Arts Press is now venturing into new possibilities by printing single author and artist books for release this year. We are hard at work! See our website for our new titles. We have twelve books we are currently working on that will be sold online and in books stores worldwide.

We also saw you in Seattle for AWP 2023 with a booth at the book fair and will follow up at AWP 2024 in Kansas City, Missouri.

We're also excited to announce our Poetry Prize in honor of Theatre Visionary Reza Abdoh; Queen Kimberly Jae Tofu Ink Arts Press Poetry Prize Winner in Honor of Reza Abdoh ***Domestic Violence Respectability Politics; The Rivers Flow Not Past, But Through Use*** by Keri Rosebraugh, who won our first Art Contest and ***Vignettes From an Only Daughter Who is Now a Wife*** by Tara Tulshyan, who won our first Chapbook Contest. The quality of their crafts are admirable! 2022 at Tofu Ink Arts Press has be nothing but amazing! We appreciate all of our supporters.

Thank you Jojo for his selfless efforts in editing and digital magic. Without you we are nothing!

Please enjoy this 2023 selection of Tofu Ink Arts Press Volume 6.

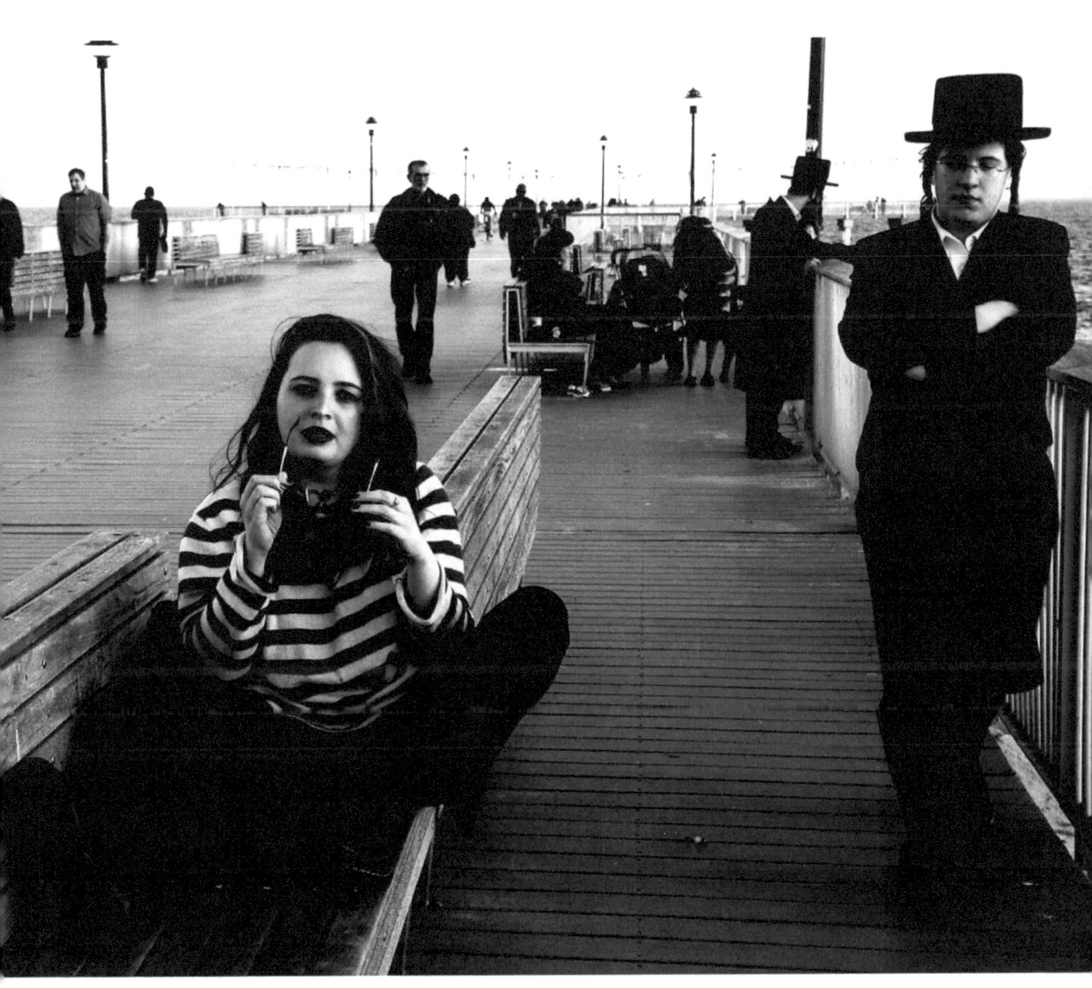

George L Stein **Coney Island Swirl**

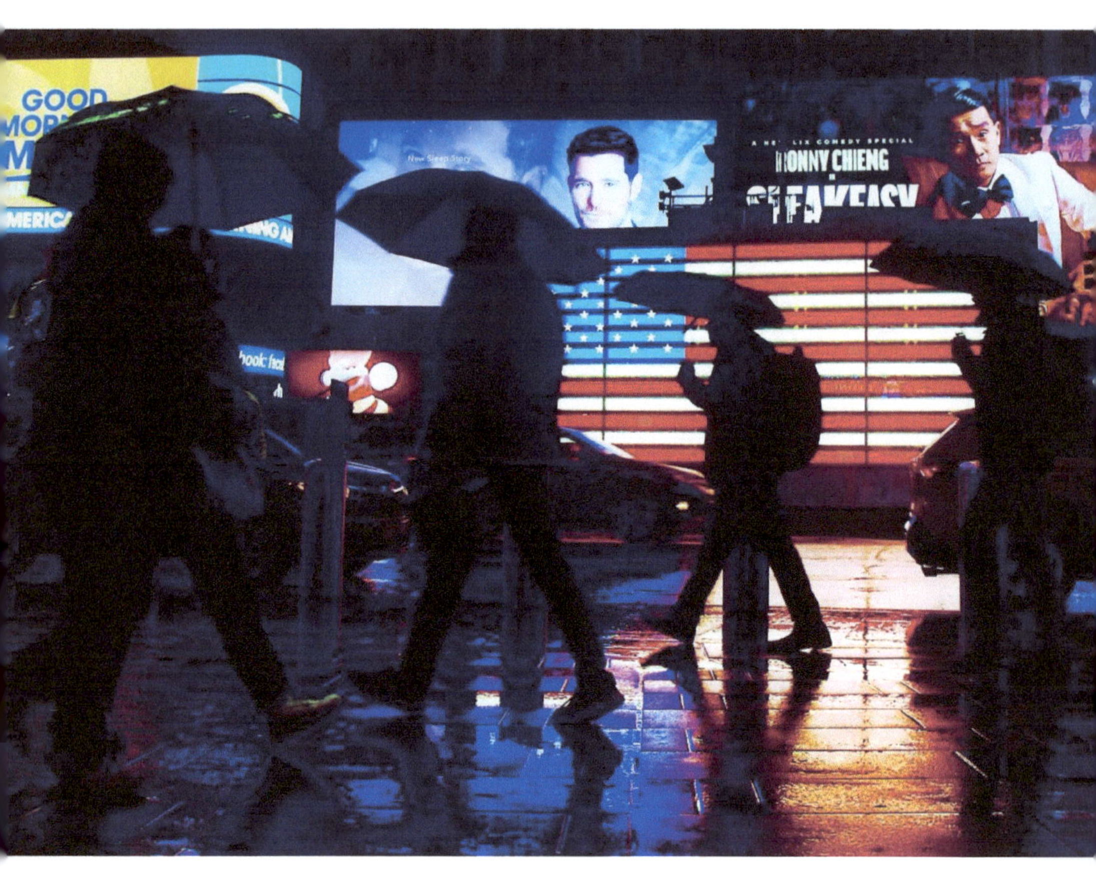

George L Stein **Weathering Umbrage**

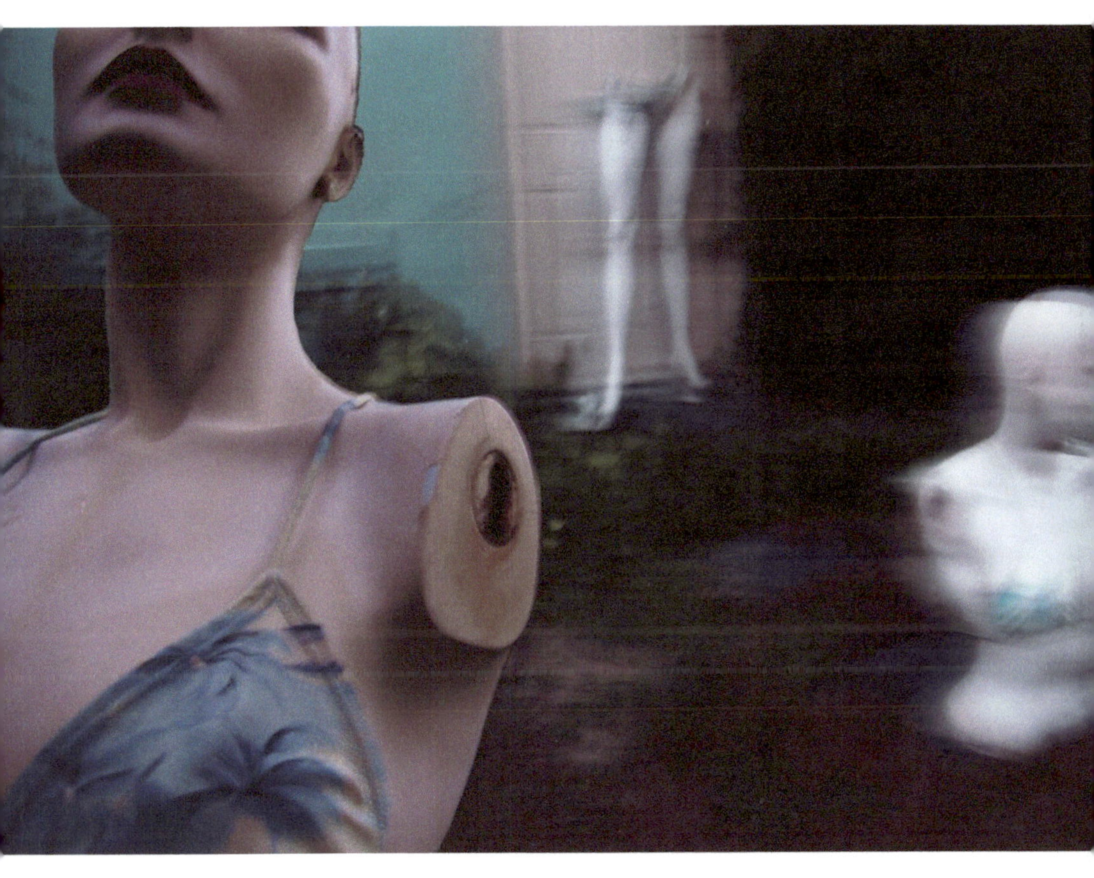

George L Stein **Aspects of Laura**

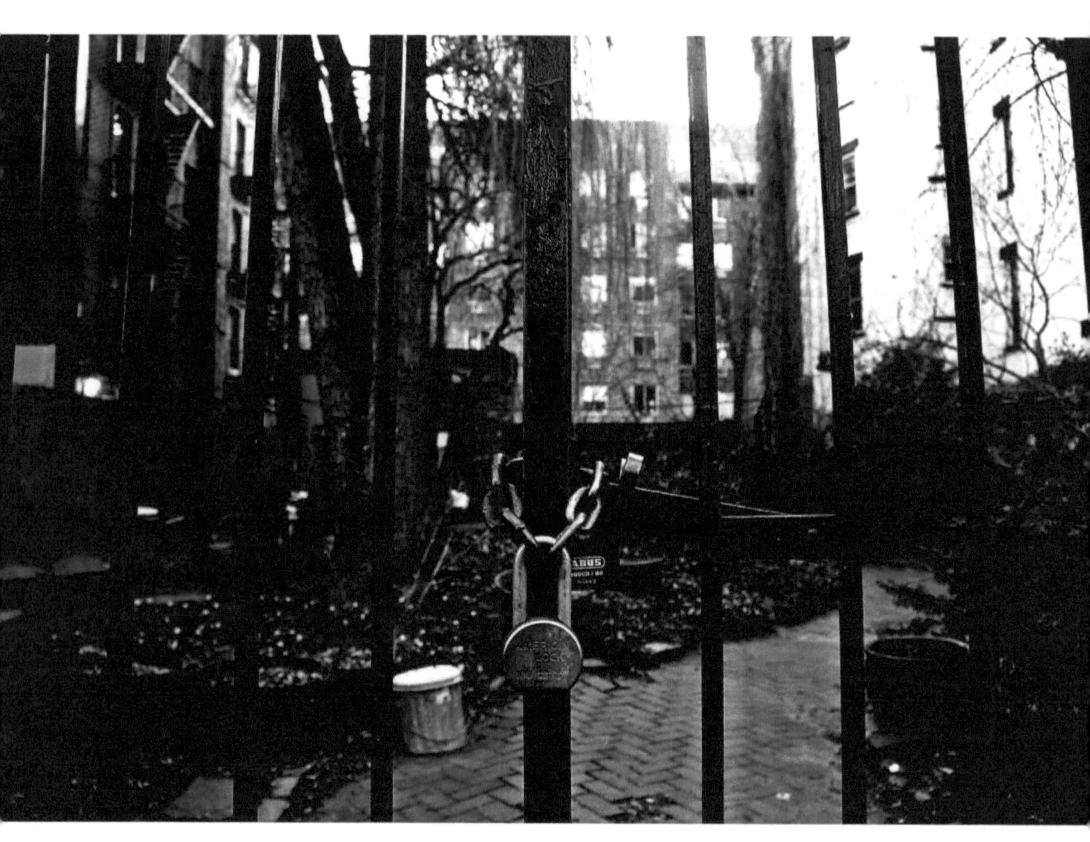

George L Stein **Structural Denial**

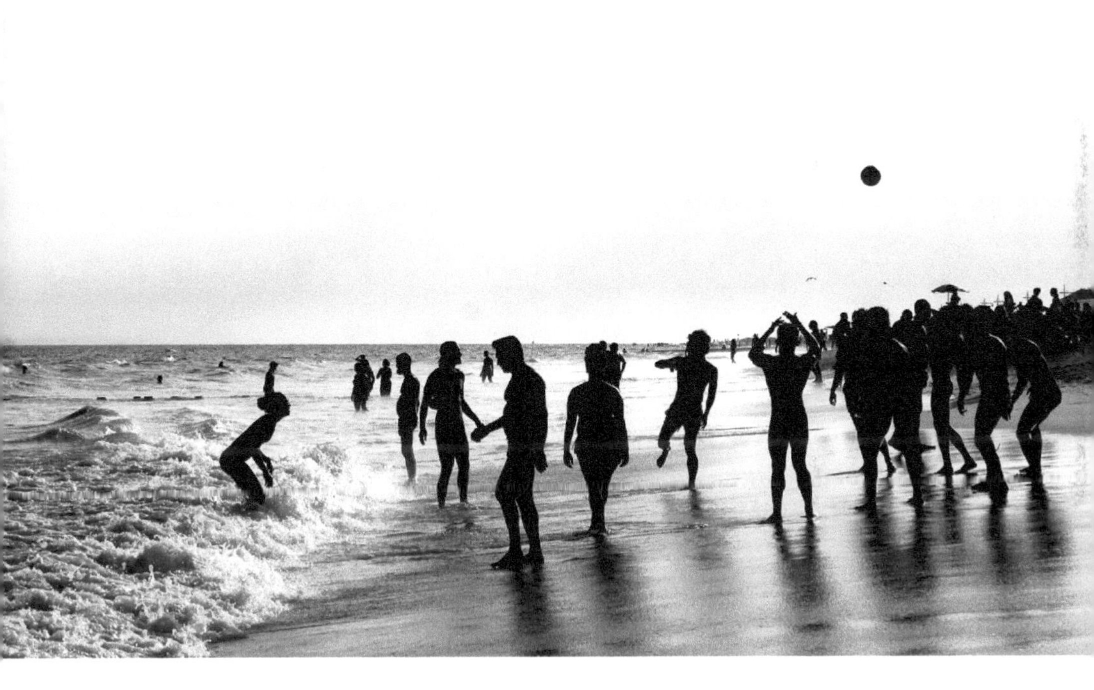

George L Stein **Games**

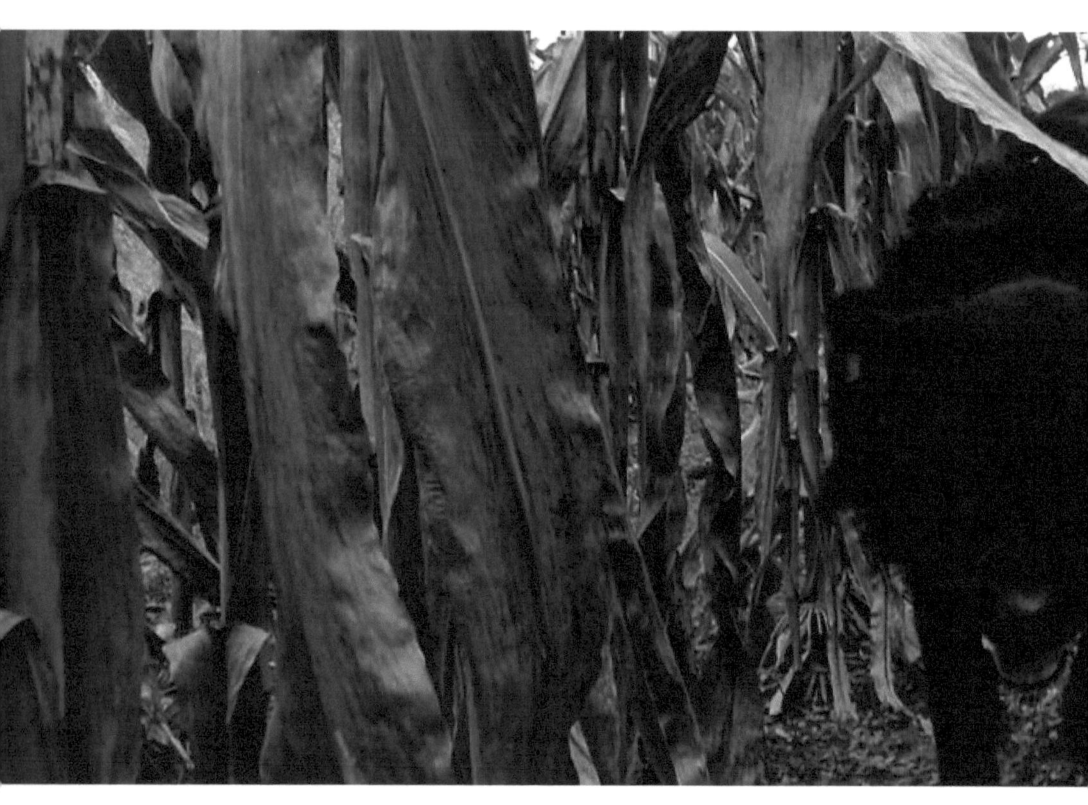

George L Stein **Feral Harvest**

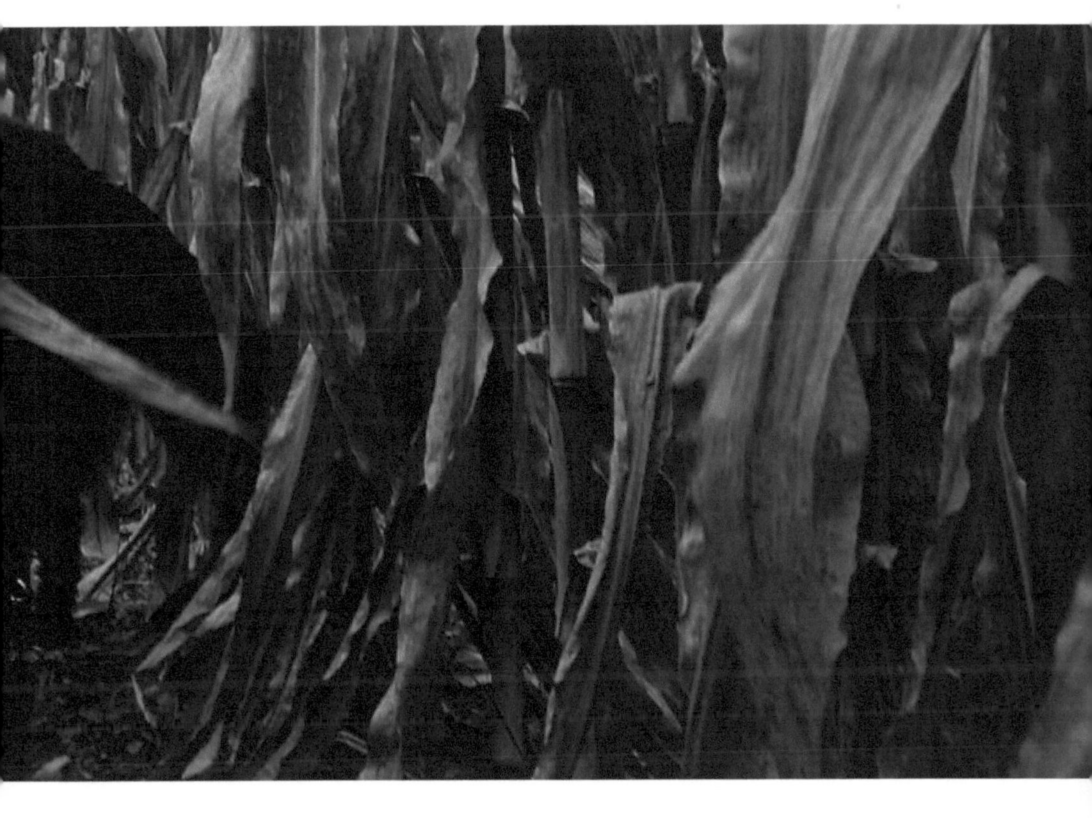

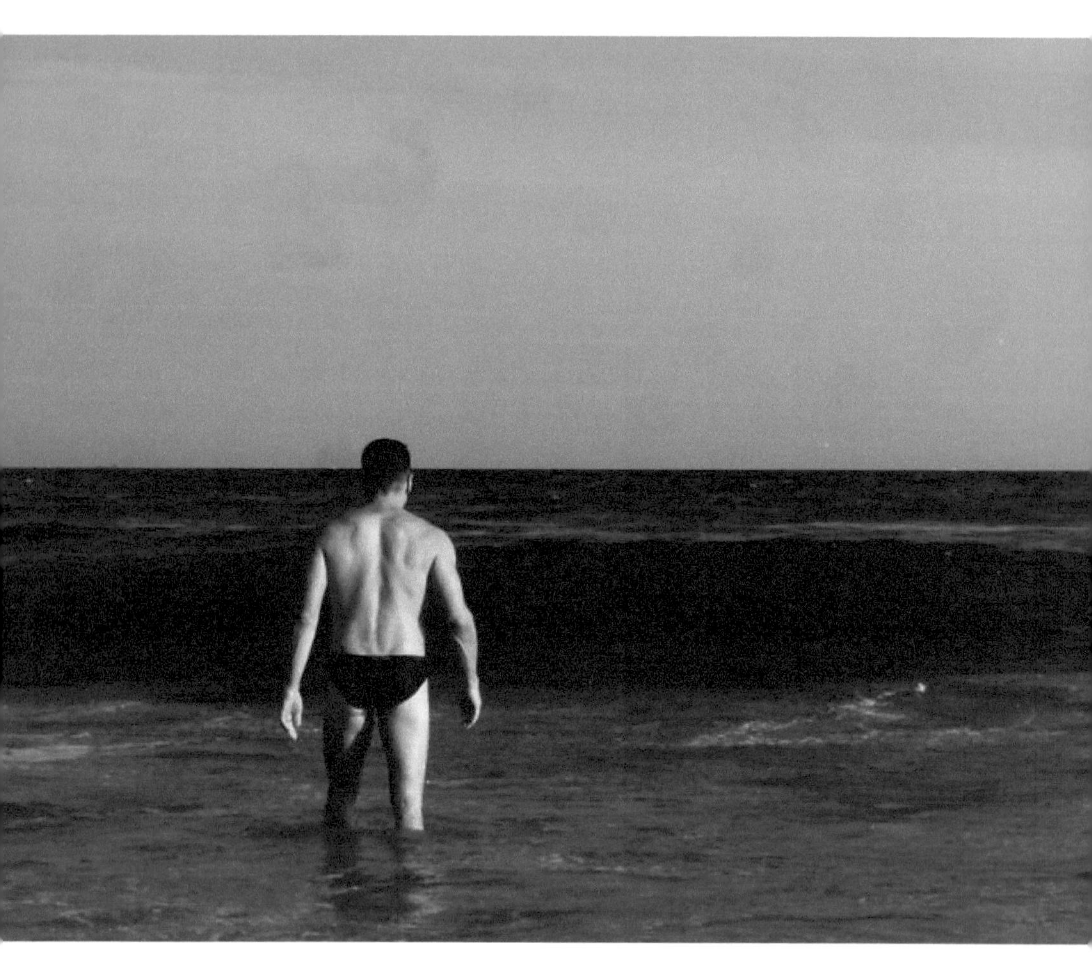

George L Stein **Everyday Expressions of the Singularity**

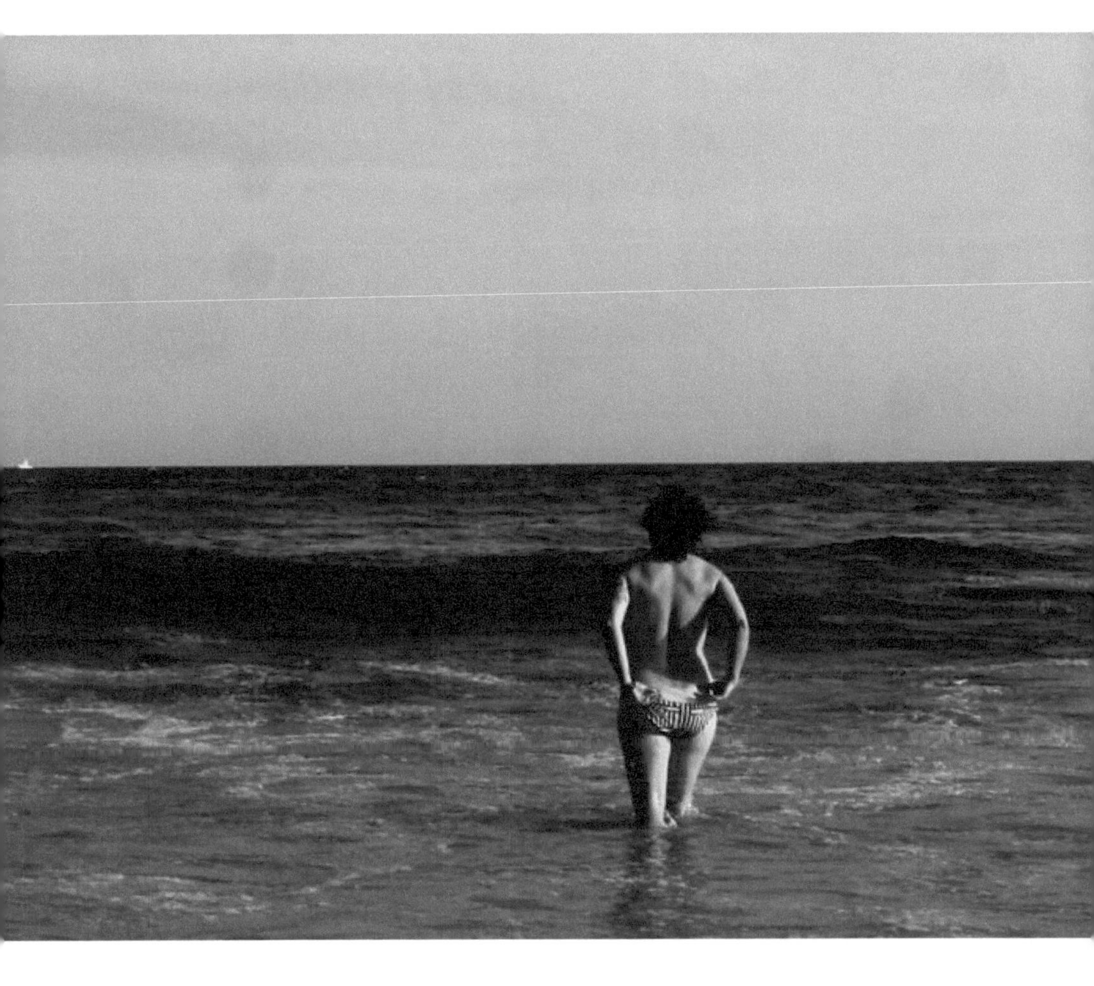

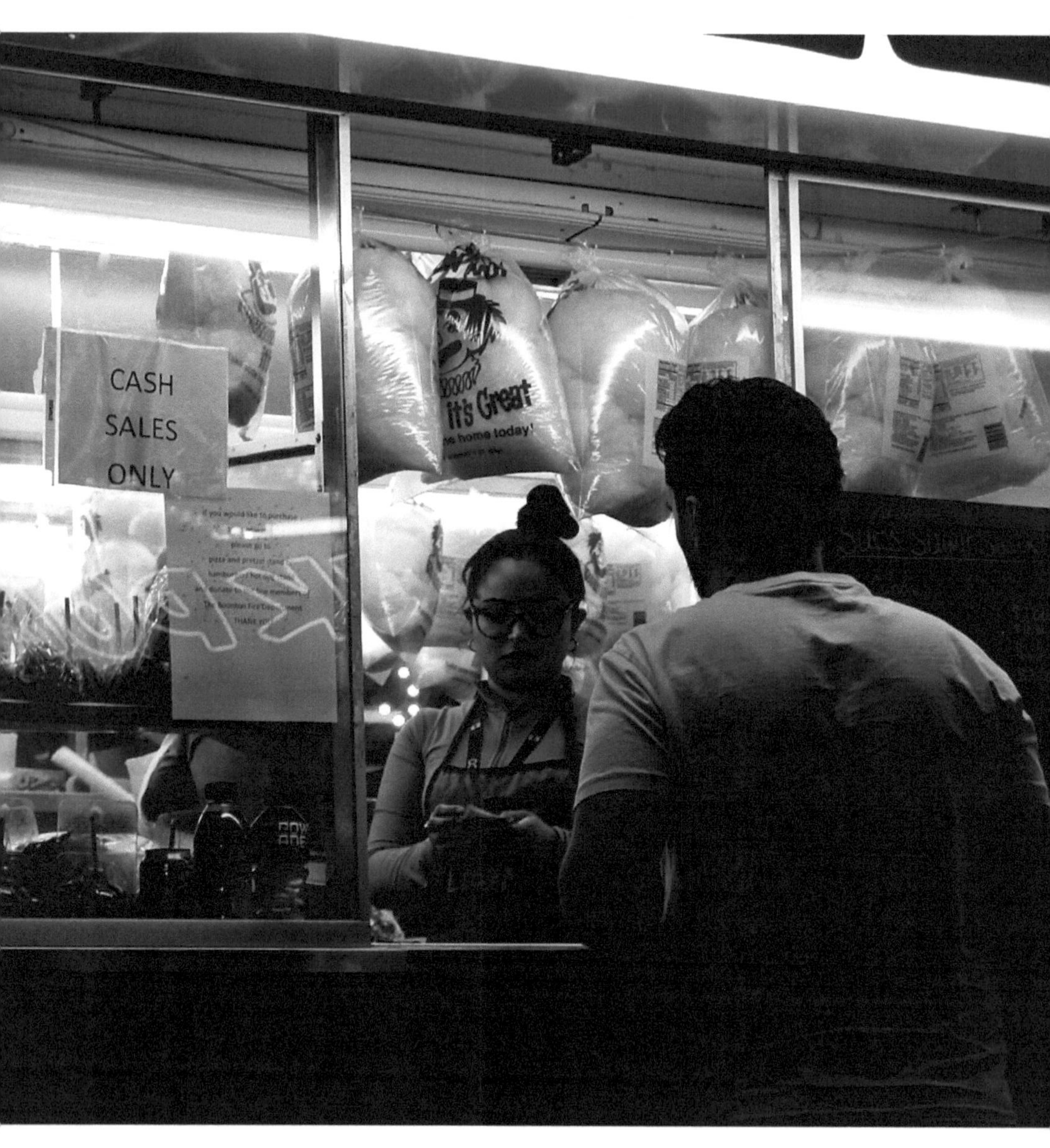

George L Stein **Cash Sales Only**

Jones Irwin
Upstream I

After Thomas Kinsella

Arising to meet us with light
That still quivered confusing in
Another guise we might think
This light was darkening more

Again, we set out our weapons drawn
We thrust ahead unifying our quest
The segment parts remained fragile

Where we looked downstream undone
Or only half-undone we hung to the water
Swimming like latter day saints

With no religion and let the prayer
Be a tension of our soul dark waters
No door would open the world

Fell down again thick slopes
Seemed labyrinthine I thought
About previous loves crawling

Across the river floor like pike is
Love a kind of cage has our love
Collapsed like a half-eaten half-

Rotten frightener of children you could
Tell my co-shadow murmured by the
Stigmata on my palms that I was born

For terror and the cold of hell is a
Balm for those of us who knew now
Know no different from birth

Jones Irwin
Berryman In Dublin

I'm just pouring whatever
I possibly can into the
one glass this mix of gin
and white wine is making me
feel so random that I could be
Theodore Roethke at his own
wake.

Jones Irwin
An Irishman In Manchester The Night The Queen Died

Innocent your honour I wasn't
even close when the Queen passed
if yes on the same land mass this
evening at Piccadilly Station there is
a kind of hush truth be told even Sinn
Féin liked her in inverse to the disrespect
for the new King but tonight is about marking
a loss which even us Irish Leftists realise so let's
say down with monarchy and up with good old Liz
who's worth a pint of a Punk IPA pint on Oldham
Street in the Northern Quarter. Sláinte.

Jones Irwin
The Current
After Raymond Carver

These fish that come to me at
all hours of the night have a
history in disparate terrorist
groupings. The Plaice for example
learnt Spanish in Mexico and fought
the Americans until all his compatriots
had been decapitated. The John Dory spent
time moving back and forth across the Irish
border for the INLA until he became unhappy
with the misleading reading of Trotsky. The female
Trout swapped allegiances between Combat 18 and
various Dutch neo-fascist factions until she ran out
of water. I find each of them admirable in their
conviction if foolhardy and with a tendency to
dogmatism. I just wish they'd keep better hours
as I'm now having to sleep through the afternoons
at work.

Jones Irwin
The Making of *Lost Highway*

Bill struck me as a guy
who could get himself
into a lot of trouble
which is surely the basis
of any good way of life
and if you take the trouble
and the time to consult the *Diagnostic
and Statistical Manual of Mental Disorders*
you will find especially the passage about
the *psychogenic fugue* instructive in a manner
that may be relatively surprising

Jones Irwin
A Poem Composed Outside *The French House*

My love comes in a glass
full of crystal meth

While Billy Childish
plays sax in Soho

Within spitshot of *The Coach and Horses*
where Freud remonstrates with Bacon

About what's on the menu
ripping off the other's cravat

As if these two were lunatic poets
knowing no better no poorer

And out of nowhere Katy Acker
turns up crying *this is no place for lovers*

Jones Irwin
We Must Wait Til Spring

To judge the march of Autumn
To see how it will all fall
Now that things have started to deconstruct
Now that Nature shouts 'Throw it out'

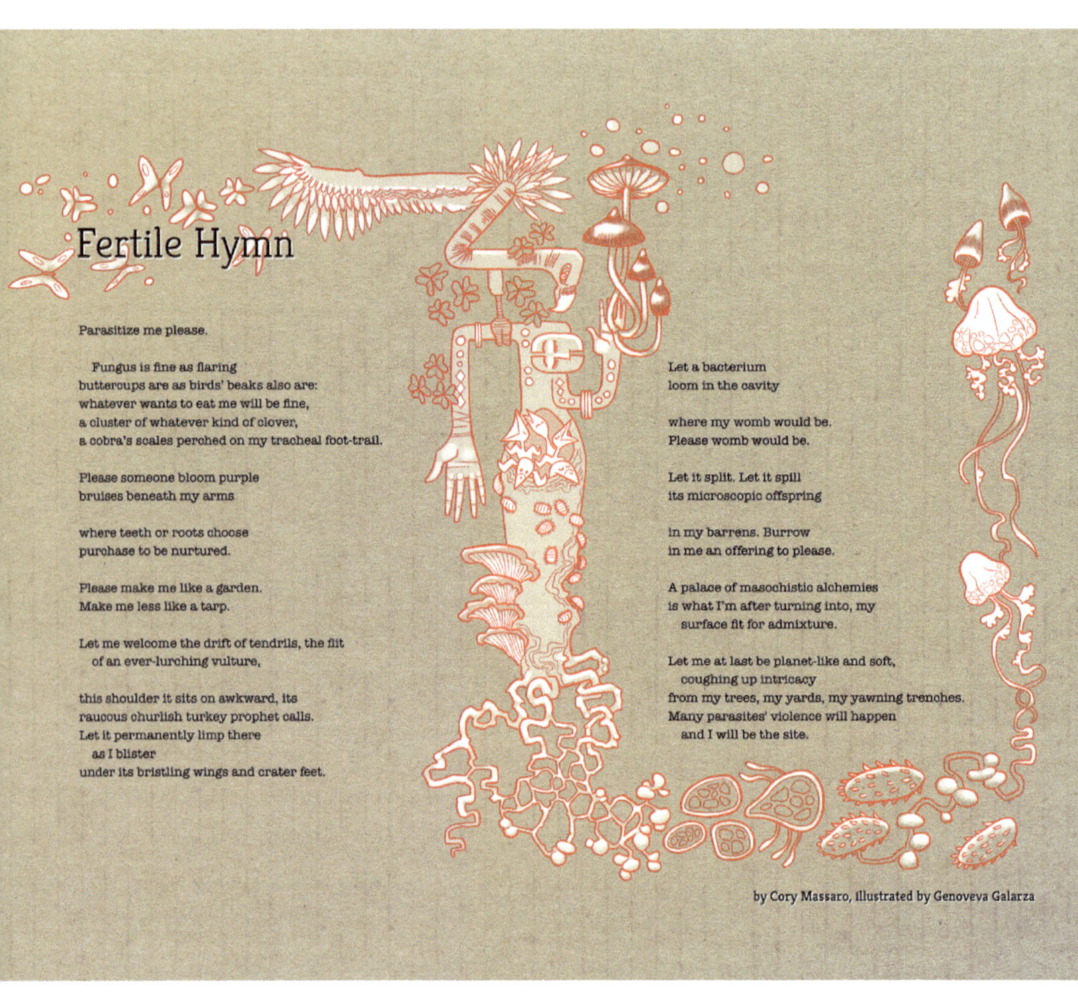

Genoveva Galarza Heredero & Cory Massaro **Ferile Hymn**

Jasper Glen
I'm content, no preference

I could eat, but I could also not eat
And that gives you a sense of
Where I am on the emotional landscape.

I can't talk. Is this an attack.
Personal opinion. Either way,
I think you're great, you're just
Not the right one for me. OK.

At least I'm facing the window.
The only question of whether I
Entered, said space cadet,
For a second you were merely
A pearl, black as the rod
You bent your mouth in.

Jasper Glen
Let's talk, I don't wanna

By bird messengers,
To our mothers.
I can't fly, sir.
Render one.
Mine is an eagle,
It has steep white hooks.
No, mine is a blue jay
Meant to mockery.
I write my messages backwards
So ze Germans can't see zem
Or even begin to undershtand.
Good impression, but deep
Down I want to lose my bluj.
I try send him far away
He jus' come back, over
And over, he won't – I
Take a vacation.

Jasper Glen
I play all childhood

Alone one year,
Hunched over the CPU
Buzz around another's
Skin-hum shyly.
I quiet but polite boy,
So easy to treat, a syndrome
Seeks outward Janets to find,
So why ply in the universe, et. al?
No, he's just a boy, ordinary
Mind. A walking pastel turned
Tapspout of poetry. Y2K
Rams of megabites
Memorialized as phrase.
And some deep thinking too,
Computers… jeez… I don't know
How they do it. Neither do we
Think machine repeats, but you're
Talking strange ways to me,
Mr. Incomprehendido.

Susannah Winters Simpson
It's The First Drink That Gets You Drunk

How was I to know the *first* wedding ring
would launch my white stockings and garter
belt permanently away from you,
 1,500 miles into the desert?
How could I know *that* diamond would place
me in none-too-clean diners and truck stops,
put me in places that served posole, chicken fried steak
and chili rellenos, or that it would keep me away
from your Elvis convertible with its lipstick red
vinyl seats, keep me from monkey sex
in the vestibule after church on any old Sunday,
would keep me from being curled inside you
on the white tile floor, and our pasta getting cold
again, in the kitchen. How was I to know
that his thin veneer of civility and chamber
music manners would evaporate under
the New Mexico noon, or that I would pine
for you in my marriage bed, wither beneath
 the shadow of Starvation Peak and that
what flamed between us could never be
contained by just one bed, one state,
or one life?

Susannah Winters Simpson
Except I Am a Knife

I thank you for leaving in the morning after sleeping with me like a spoon in a
drawer.
Thank you for pretending I am a spoon made to scoop up soups and dip into
berries. Thank you for ignoring my blade and my serrated edge, thank you for
turning a deaf ear to the ring of the whetstone in the kitchen as I sharpen
myself for the day. Thank you for all the closed doors, the spills in the fridge,
and on the floor, thank you especially for the empty toilet paper rolls and
toothpaste boxes piled in a heap next to the toilet. Thank you for not sharing
pictures of yourself or your kids, thank you for never letting any hint of an
original thought, aspiration or dream escape like steam from the corners of
your eyes. Thank you for the almost affection you gave my dogs, and the
cloying concern you aimed at me. Thank you.

Susannah Winters Simpson
Fatherly Advice Given to My Teenage Self

The front of your blouse should always
have a modest drape and never wear printed voile.
It is such a cheap looking fabric. Remember that
too much make-up and chewing gum is low class,
a little lipstick is all a girl needs.

Conduct yourself at the dinner table,
as if you are eating with the Queen of England
and tuck your pelvis in and under as you walk.
Men don't like women with opinions,
so, keep it to yourself, tone it down.
If you like a boy, touch his hand,
look into his eyes and tell him so.

You can't put bread on the table with poetry.
On this matter alone, he was right.

Harvey Humphrey
Name Yourself

I thought I hated it when someone used my name to ask something of me
whether it was something simple like pass the salt
or something more complex like vote no on parts 3b

for a second I'd stop listening when they said my name
and I had to return myself to where and when I was
I thought it was some manipulative game

trying to get my support with some personal touch
illuminated the falseness of the approach
these false friendships, conaraderie – bit much

but now I realise I was upset with the wrong part
they had my wrong name in their mouths
those incorrect referents were causing the stop-start

Now people call me Harvey because I've asked
I hear how it sounds in different voices and accents
I hear it in requests, questions, it goes by so fast

the people I care for most use my name
and the world just doesn't stop
The person right here listening is self-same

but this time I'm really listening
and I hear Harvey unfurled from friends' lips
from mother tongues, and my place in the world is repositioning

yeah of course I'll pass the salt, I'll make you a tea,
I'll vote for the motion, I'll be over later today, I'll be right here
Thanks Harvey, Cheers Harvey, Ta Harvey, Thanks

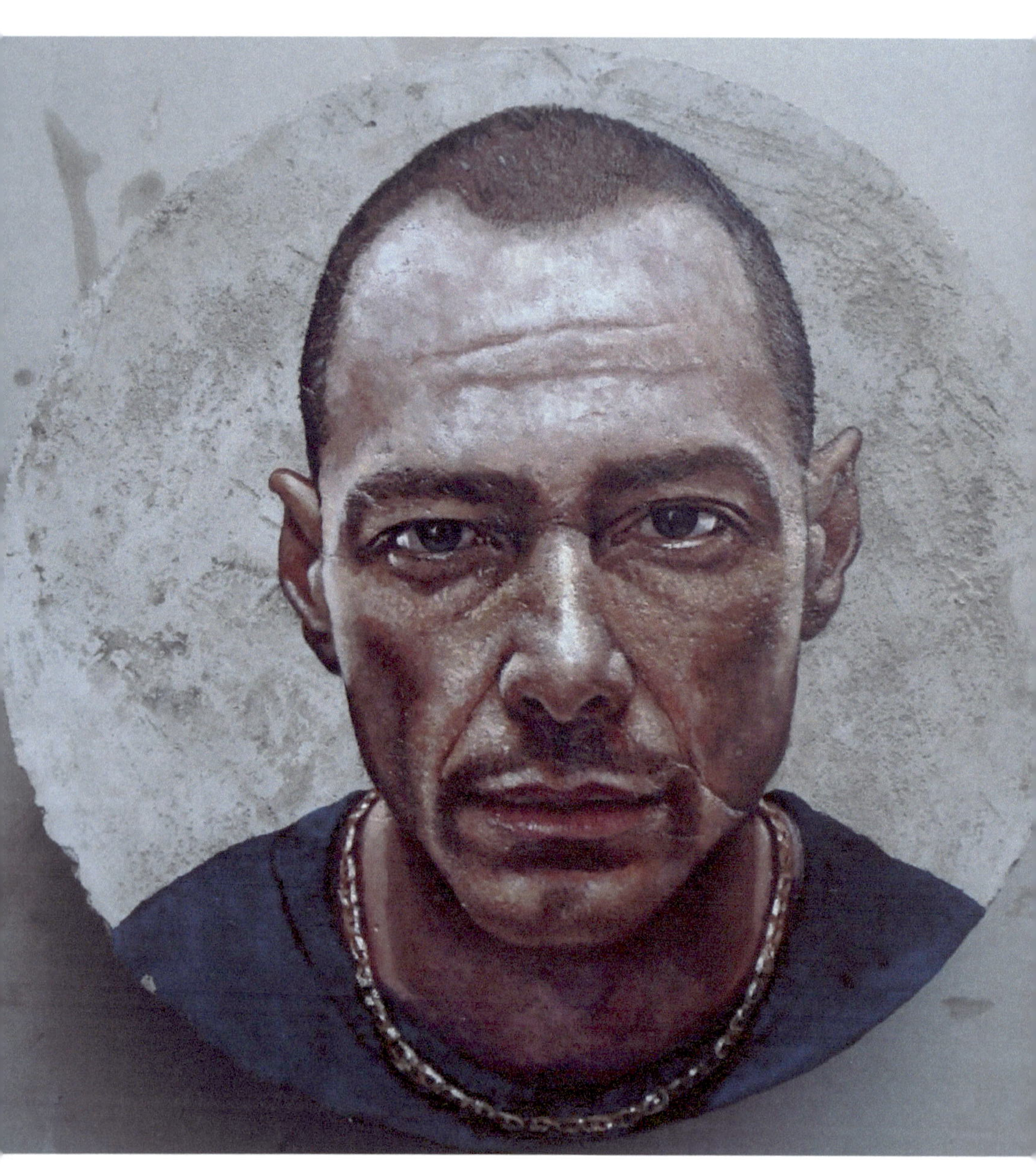

Mario Loprete **Untitled**

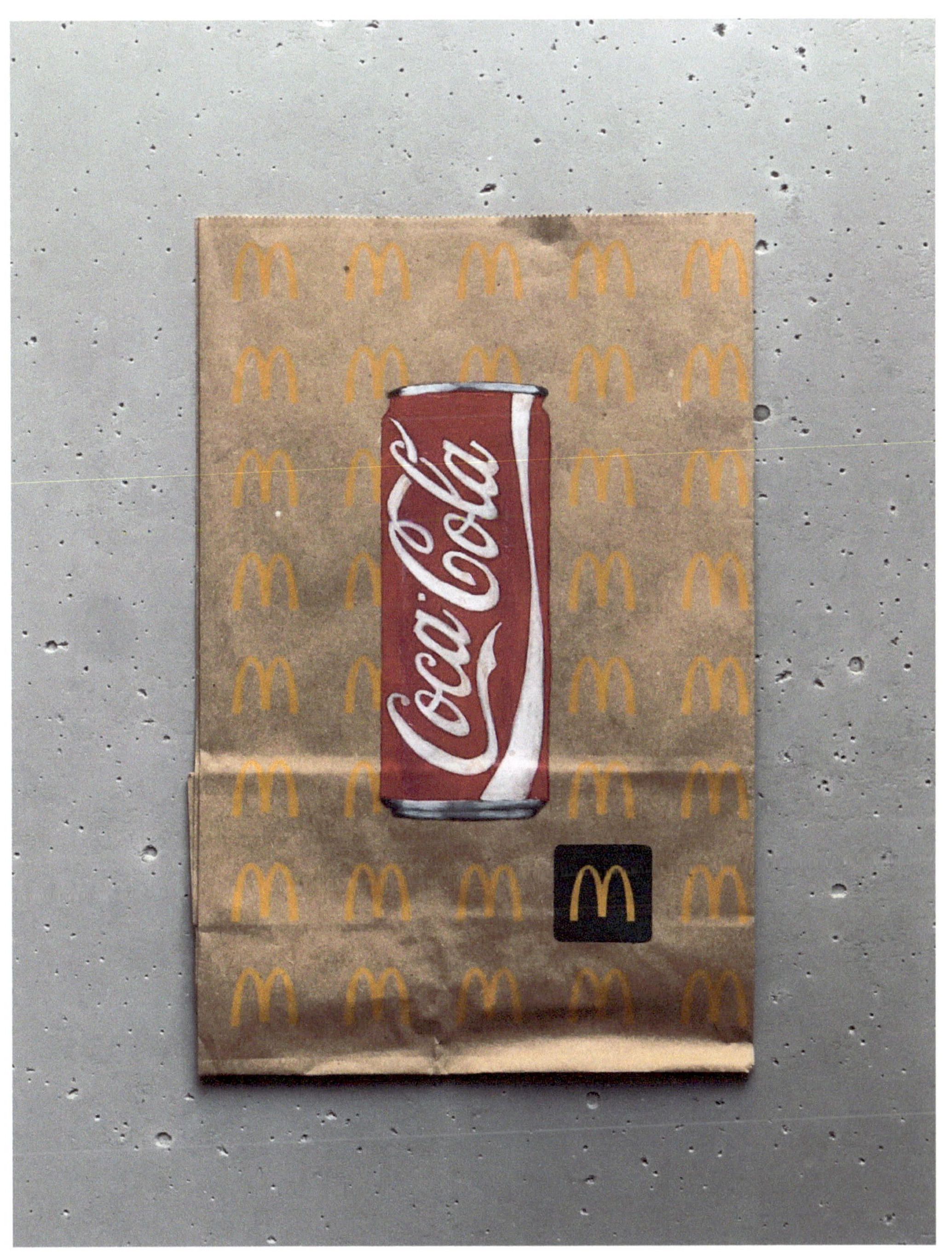

Mario Loprete **Untitled**

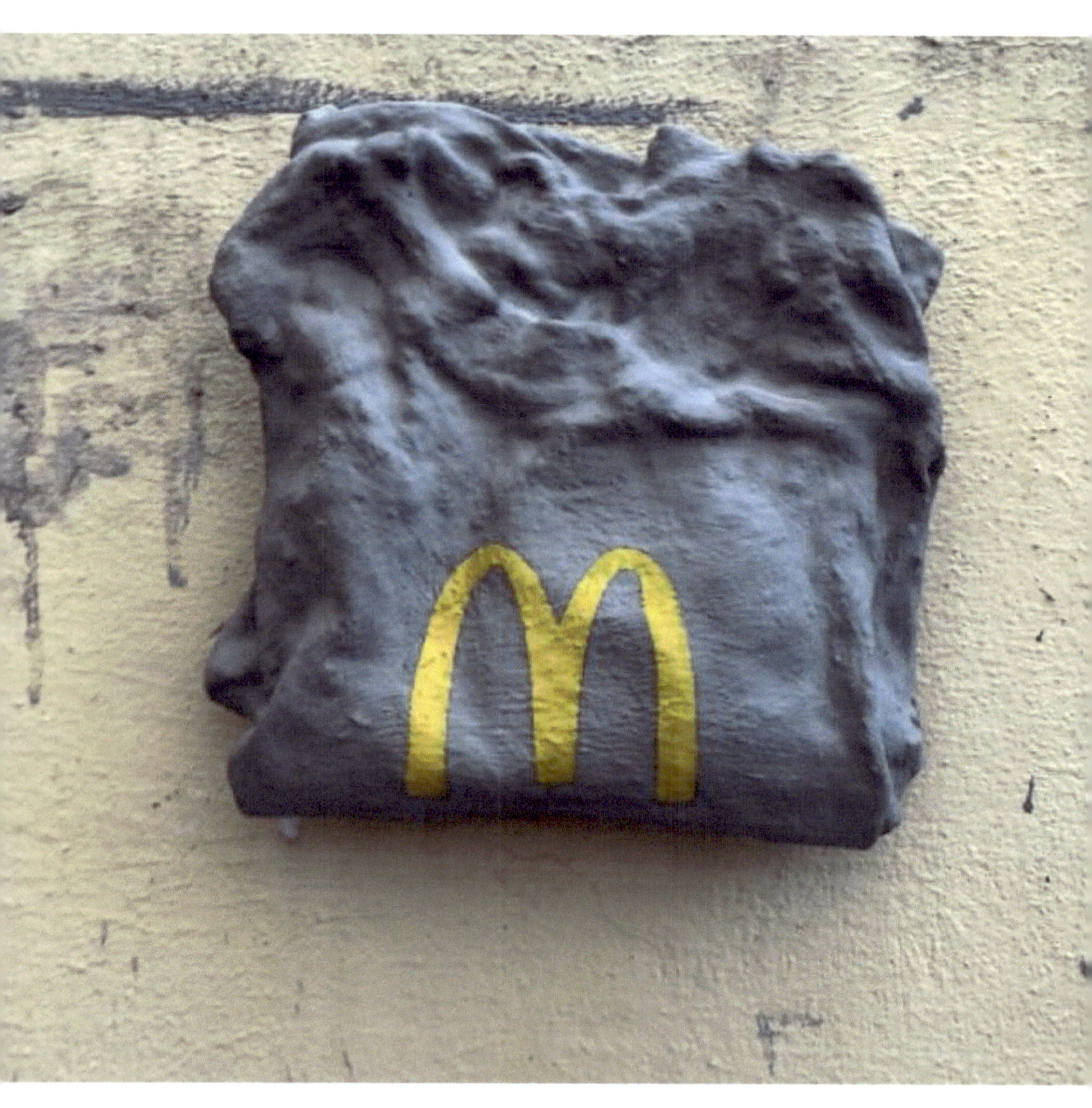

Mario Loprete **Untitled**

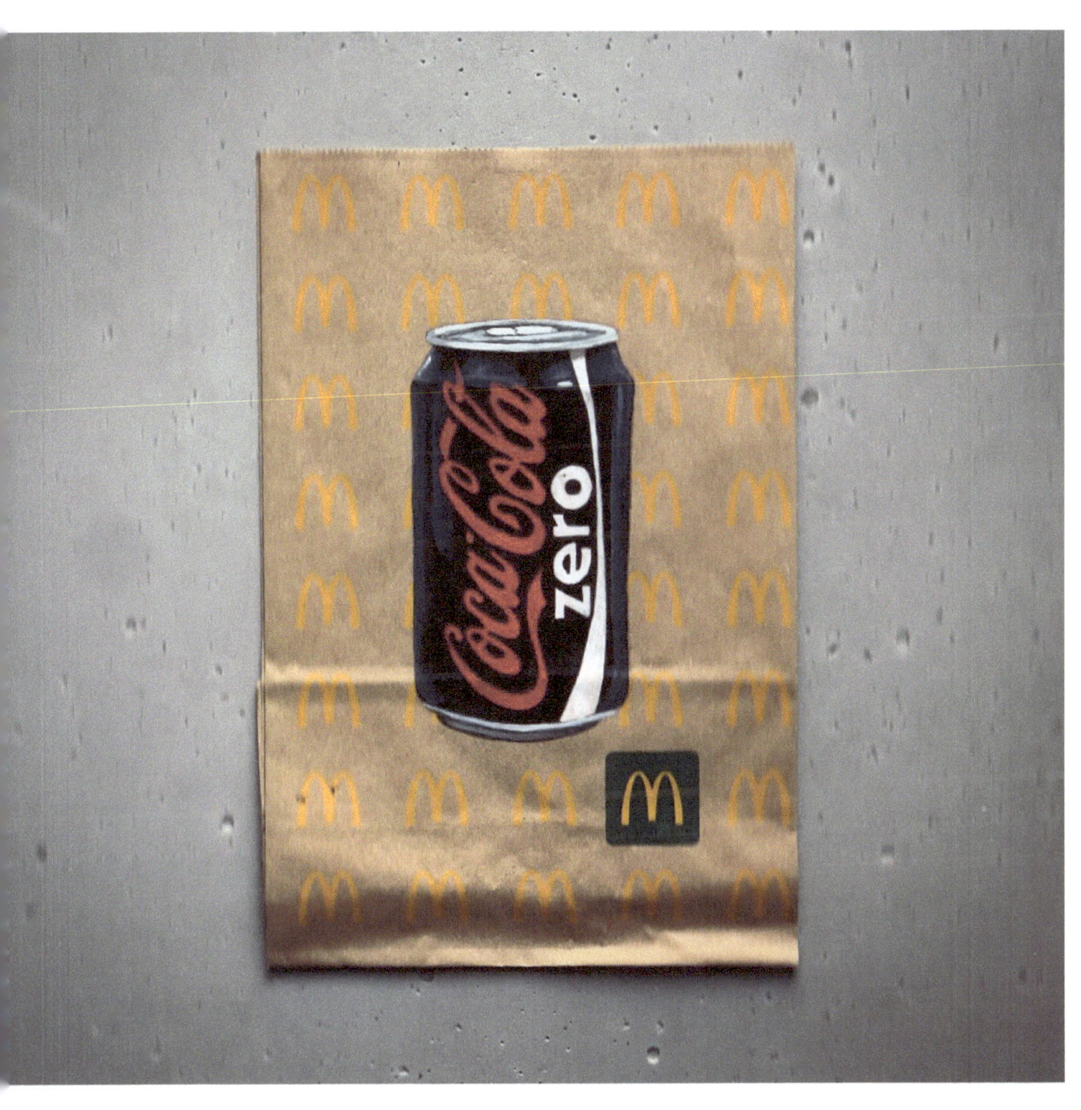

Mario Loprete **Untitled**

Jon Lawrence
The New School

I tour the trauma aquarium.
Men flap to bedpans,

embryos in fluorescent tanks
pulse like jellyfish.

My forearms bath in blue
shimmer of dark seas.

Wailing mothers,
babies plucked from wombs.

Teenagers scratch faces
in bathroom mirrors.

Men look for themselves
in red windows.

Touch pools of bodies
slapped like bags of wine.

Children out the door for g-force bomb blasts
where they sift shrapnel like gold.

Suspended in pressurized chambers
we snap pictures to send our bones through clouds

waiting for tick mark gratifications
while women bleed through teeth.

Plunge yourself deep into a caricature of skin.
Let it wrap like cellophane.

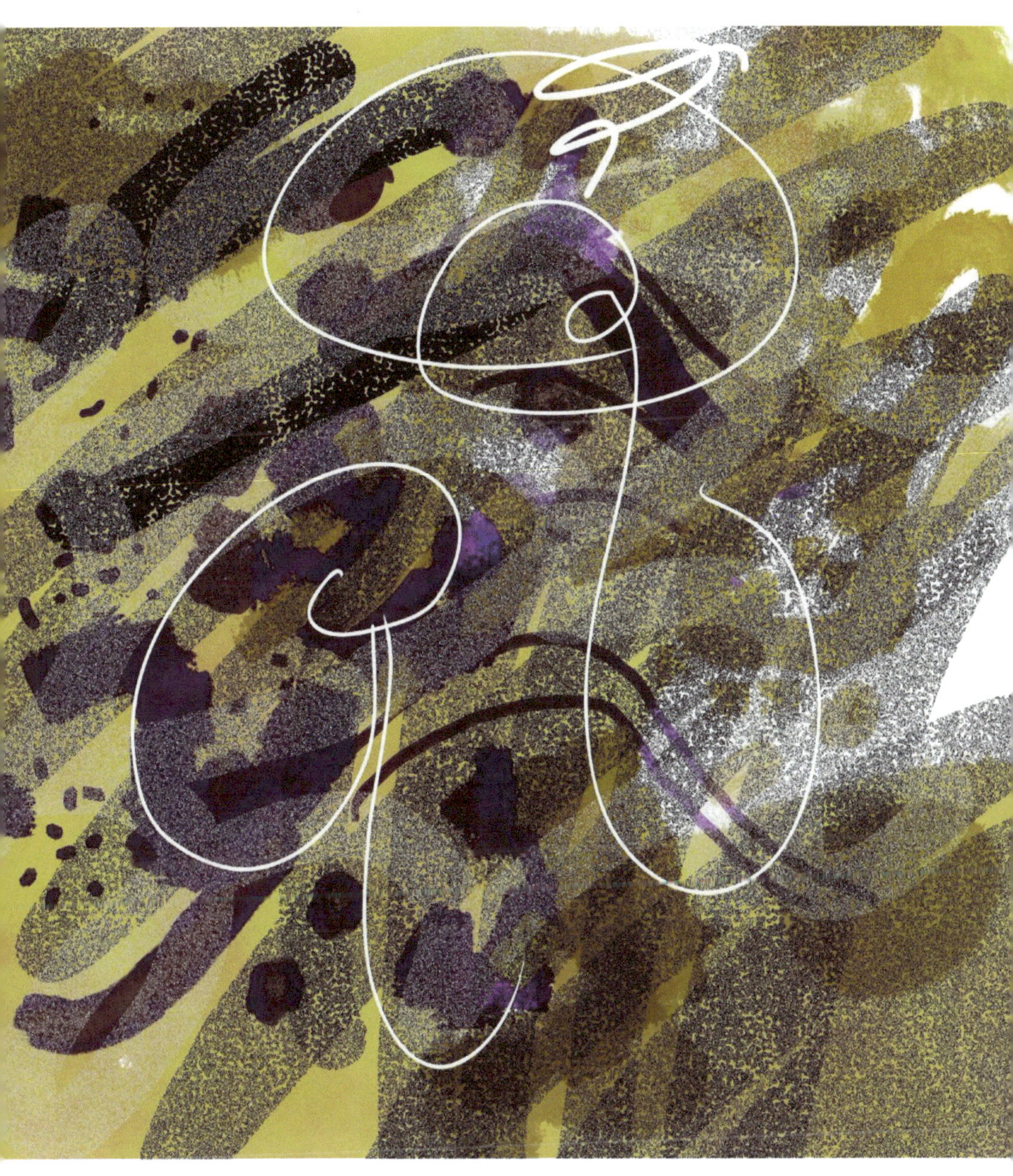

Dana Rivera **Zing**

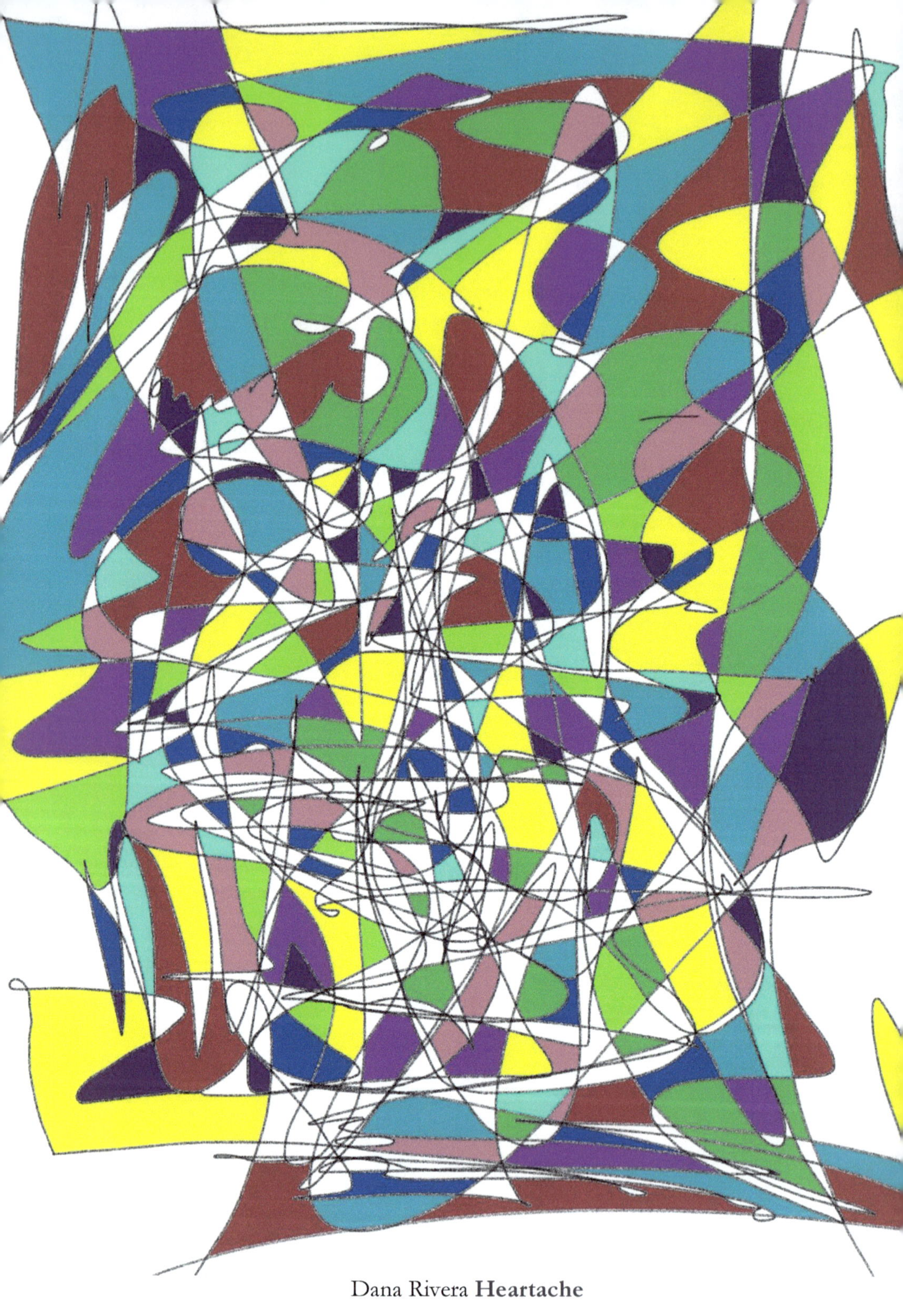

Dana Rivera **Heartache**

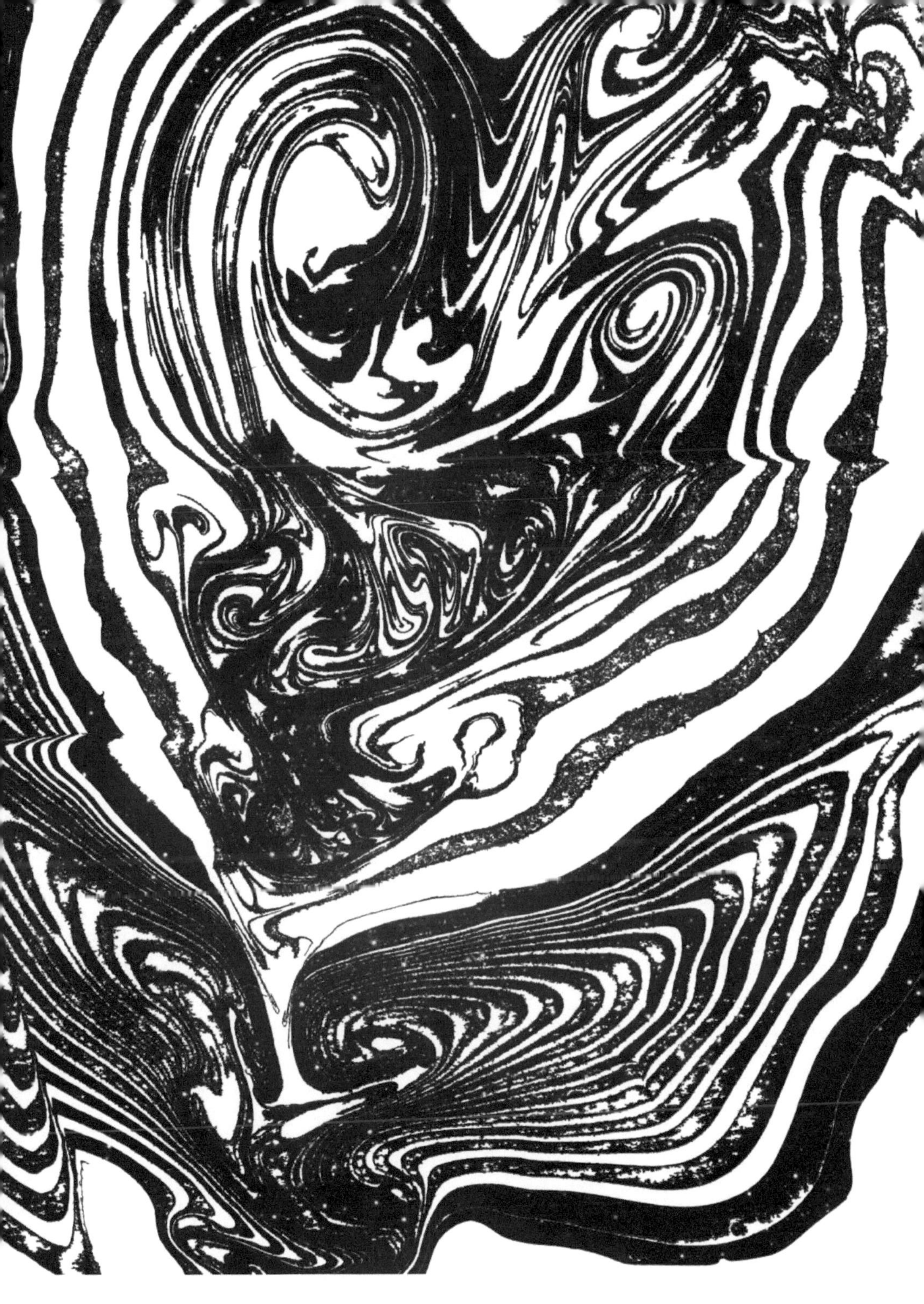

Dana Rivera **Water Marble Four**

Miles Weber
Conspiracy Analyst

— Gore Vidal

The police in Vegas,
by giving federal agents
a tongue bath,
confirmed the universal hunch.
The shooter acted alone
the FBI report concluded,
despite decoy shootings
further down the strip.

And the pizza restaurant.
Another lone gunman, on a rescue mission,
emptied his weapon into the floorboards.
Makes sense. Children are adept at dodging bullets.
You must tell me which bureaucrat writes these scripts.
One round, we're told, pierced the casing
of the restaurateur's laptop.
The famous blonde television journalist
who interviewed this afficionado
of off-color jokes
about naked tykes
didn't press him
on that serendipitous occurrence.

I've not spoken of these crimes
till now. I've tried lying low.
If government agents
are tracking me,
their interest stems
from previous entanglements.
My siblings never respected
my views on cosmic visitors
and I refused to bend
the knee, that's all.
We can't come to an understanding
about my medications, either,
and their quick fix
is institutionalization.

How the tables have turned. Now
former presidents and former presidents'
wives tout government photographs
proving pilots don't cross our airspace alone.
But my obligation
is to question every lie
the ruling class espouses.
Experience, when government and press align,
has taught us this.
Perhaps there have been
no alien sightings,
just exceedingly agile weather balloons.
Where does that leave us in the universe?

I offer one assurance:
If newspapers report
I offed myself,
the White House got to me.
I can't hang to death
from a hotel doorknob.
But were I to become
depressed and suicidal,
our missing soulmates
throughout the galaxy
would be the final straw.

Joey Salomone
worm food

the truth is supposed to dirt,

       dig down
              deep

and pull out the worms and earth, but don't trust the birds

surrounding your heart, take your pill treats or else the eating

away inside of a tin can composed of self-esteem continues,

in leu of a loss, devise a dynamic solution seeking compromise and

take down your obituary reflecting tirelessly on phrases of

resilience shifting the narrative of life as a positive participant,

eliciting questions and selling false hope as you awake to a

grim destination,

shovels cutting worms in half as they unearth and

engulf you in your new shrine.

Joey Salomone
the collective

american adolescents attempting acceptance are actively addicted

growing up between barstools, tight jeans and stale nuts forgetting

the system at the potluck, you fucked it up paper cup

collective human ignorance is no excuse to ignore dignity

I yell at traffic lights while giving in to the dance company

inside my chest shimmering rage and firebombs as

video games replace the american buffalo,

a man plays violin under the blue skyline with yellow windows and

stars impossible to tell them apart from caveman markings on

a wall you see a poorly choregraphed fight scene as the

village idiot tries to put out the flame with an empty

extinguisher.

Brian L. Jacobs
Jarred

jarred
directionless

traumatisms
successions

elocutionary synergy
liason'd

to the totality
world

Brian L. Jacobs
Skirmish

endlessly un root
the soil

mute emerges a lesson
of attached selves

the taciturn receptacle
versus your mounts subsists

fell drunk
amid the skirmish

Brian L. Jacobs
In the Forgotten Earth of Our Voices

derision sings
its tango

pass through bodies
unemployed

exalted
secret liberty

no community here
be stripped of its individualities

extracted against
this drive

dead
scorched

in the forgotten earth
of our voices

Brian L. Jacobs
Requiems for Our Conveniences

requiems
of renunciations

requiems
of our conveniences

relish
dithering things

without conducting
narratives for our conveniences

Jaap Blonk
Vibrant Islands

"Vibrant Islands" is a cycle of 9 pieces for acoustic vocal performance, made in 2015. Each movement consists of a number of "islands" containing phonetic signs, many of which were invented by myself. For many years I have been working on my personal extension of the International Phonetic Alphabet: BLIPAX (BLonks IPA eXtended). In the performance the islands can be visited in any order, and repeatedly as well. In every score of the cycle the coastal lines have a different form, for instance angular, crenelated, straight or rounded, according to the prevalent sound character of the movement. For a performance of this work an intimate room with good acoustics works best. A complete performance of "Vibrant Islands" can last between 18 and 45 minutes.

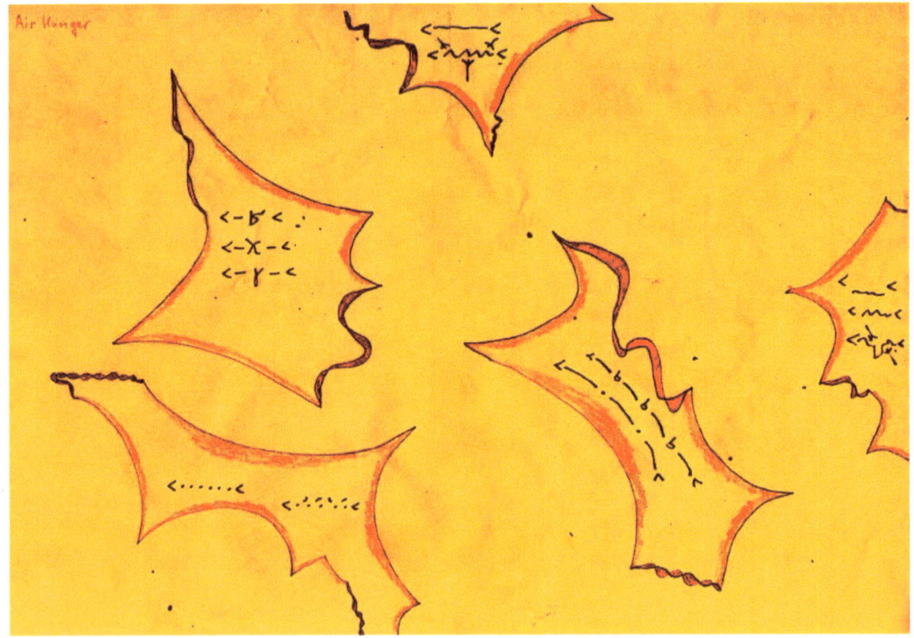

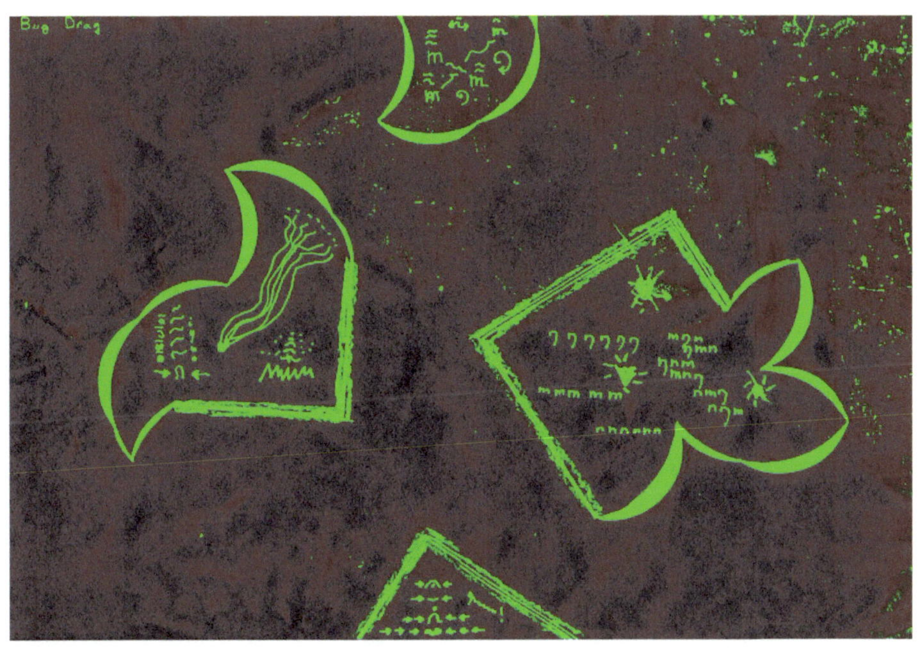
Bug Drag

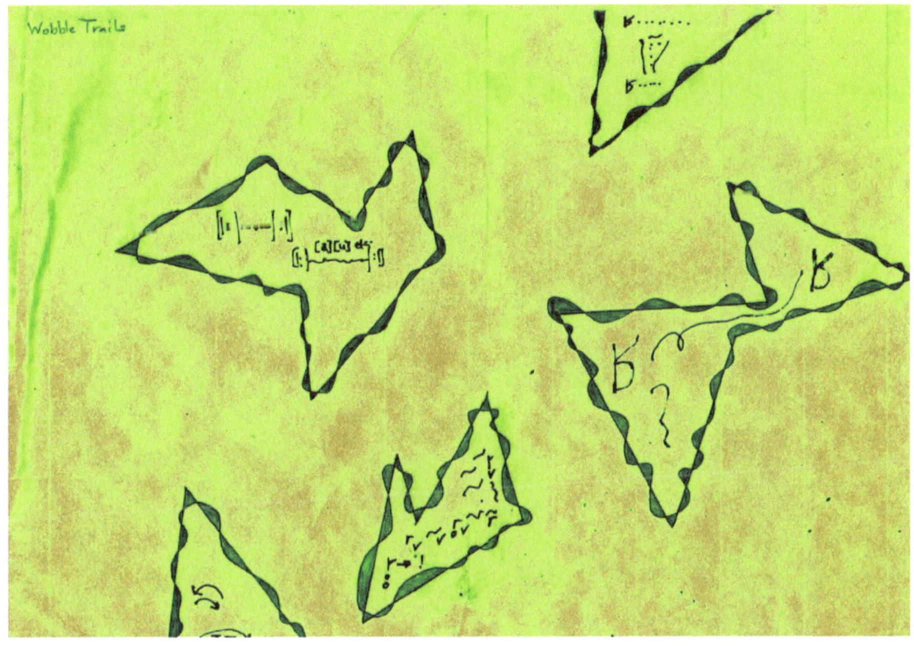
Wobble Trails

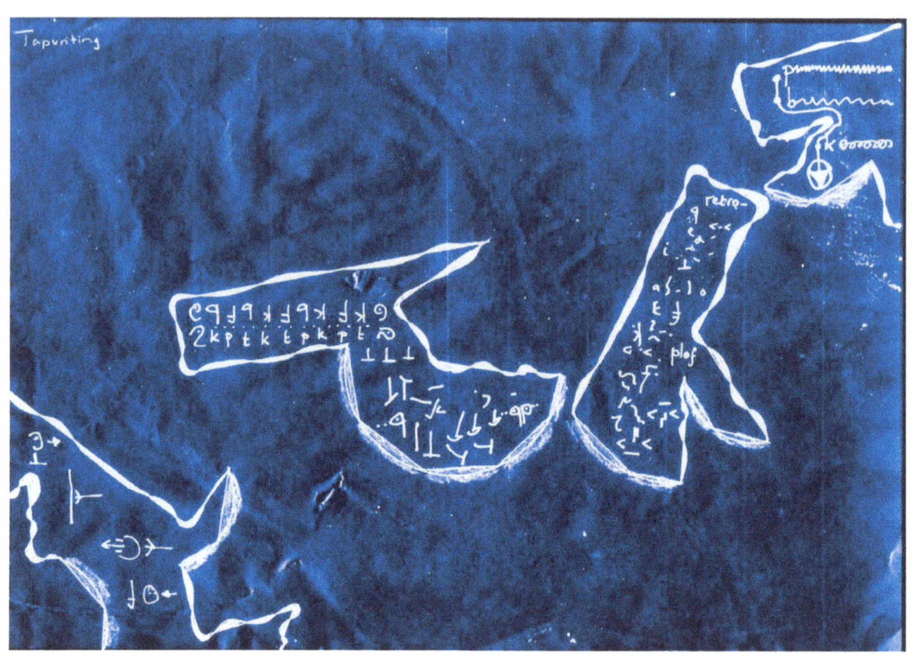
Tapwriting

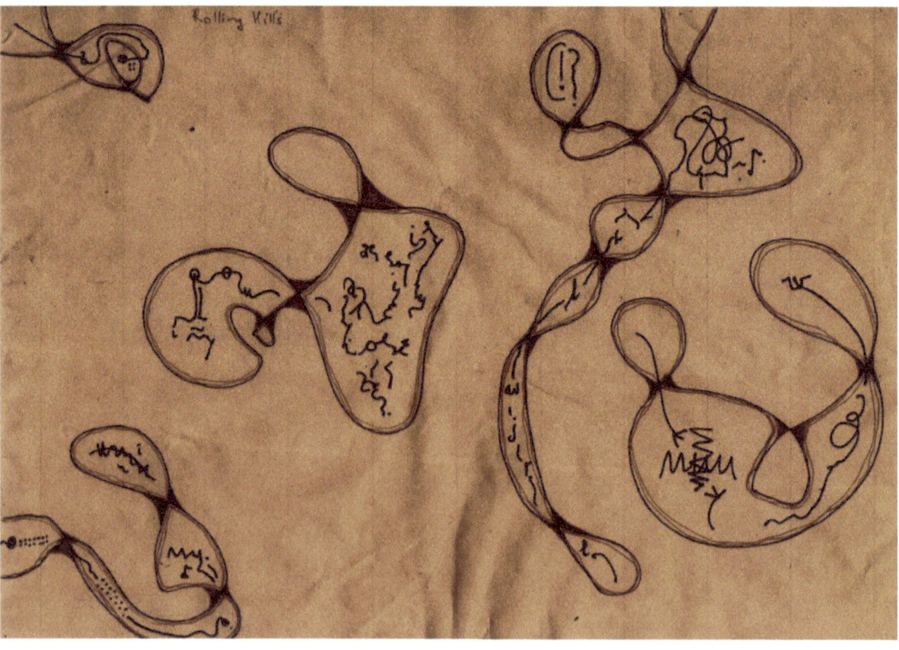
Rolling Kills

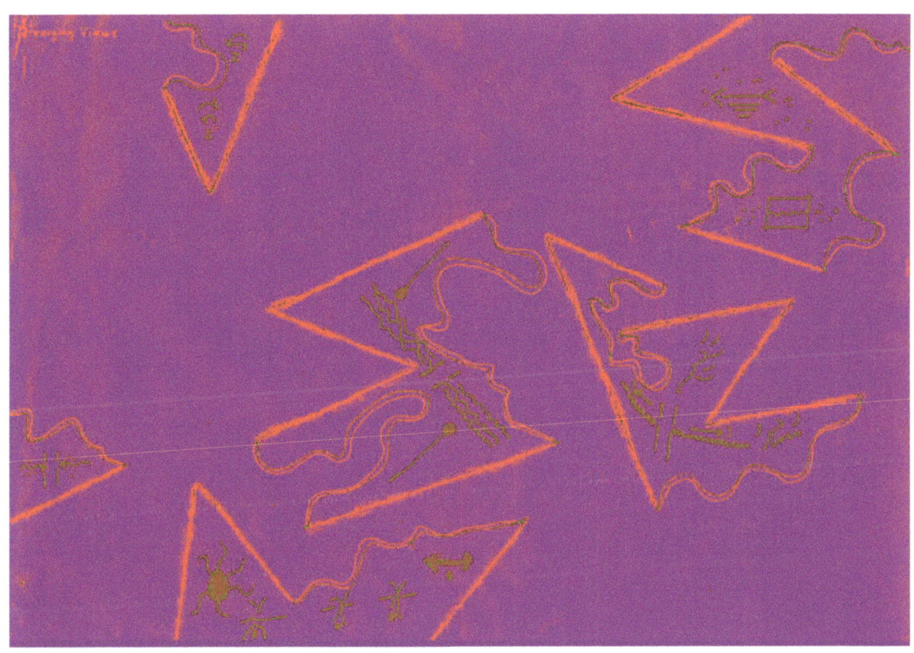

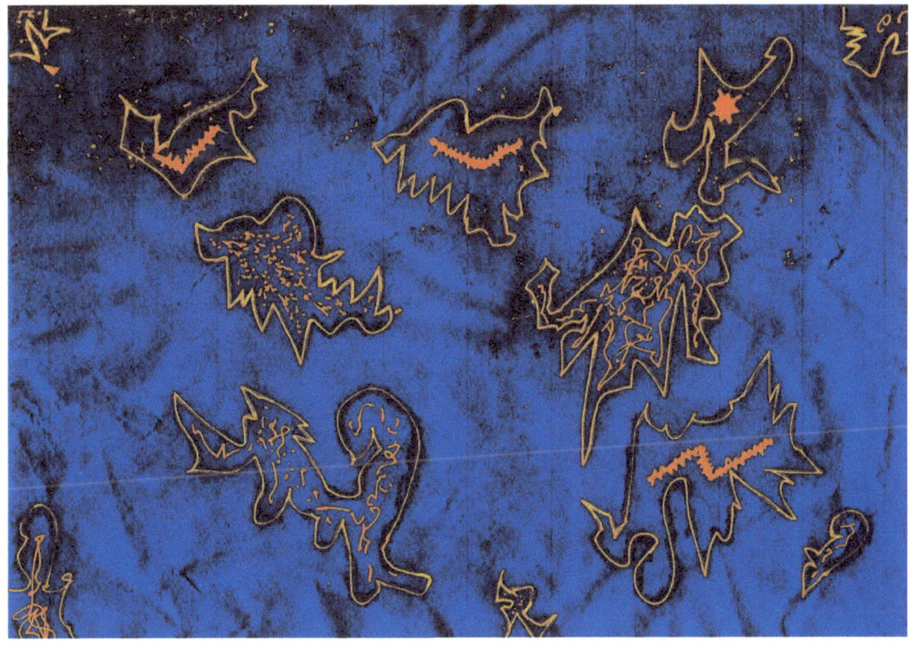

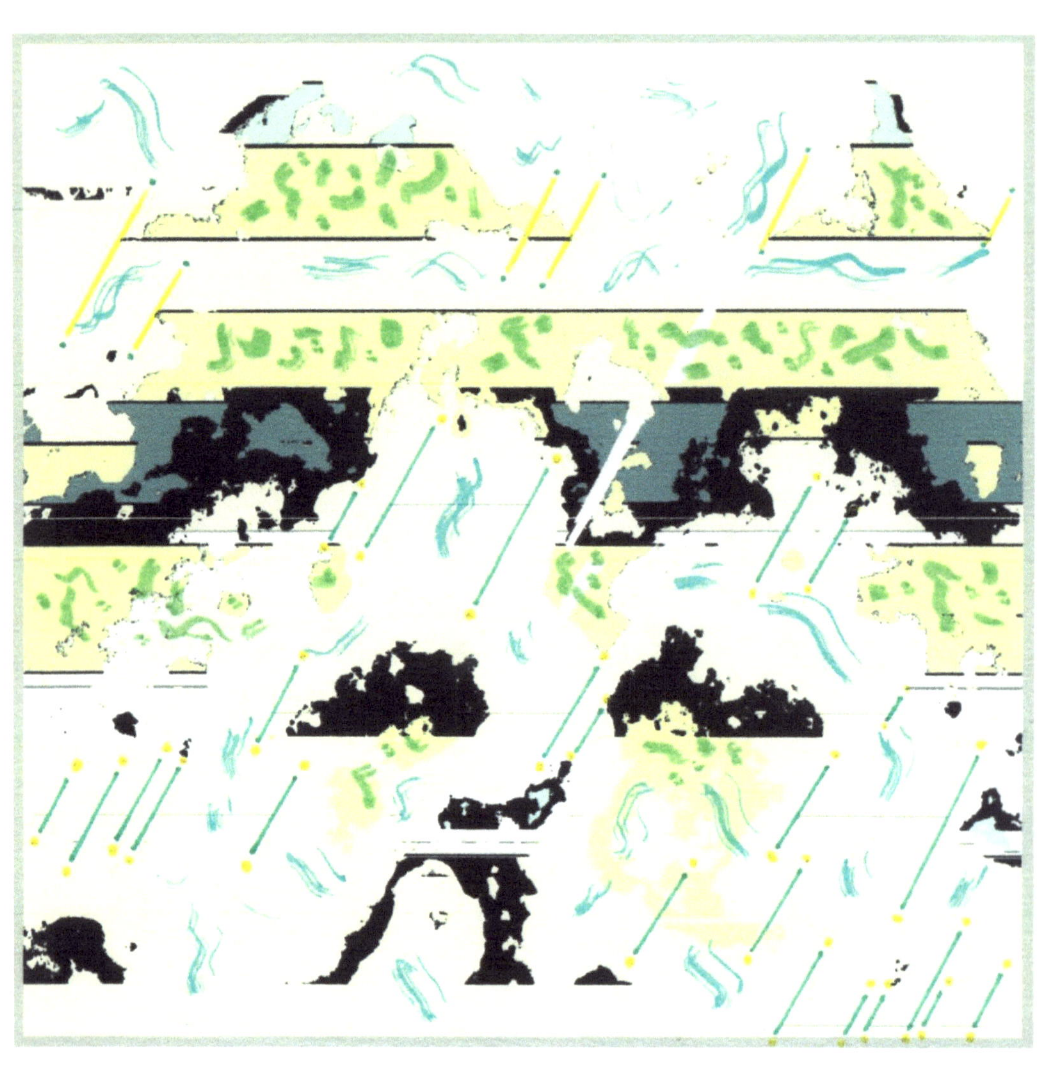

GUTTRIX
Phonetic Etude #5

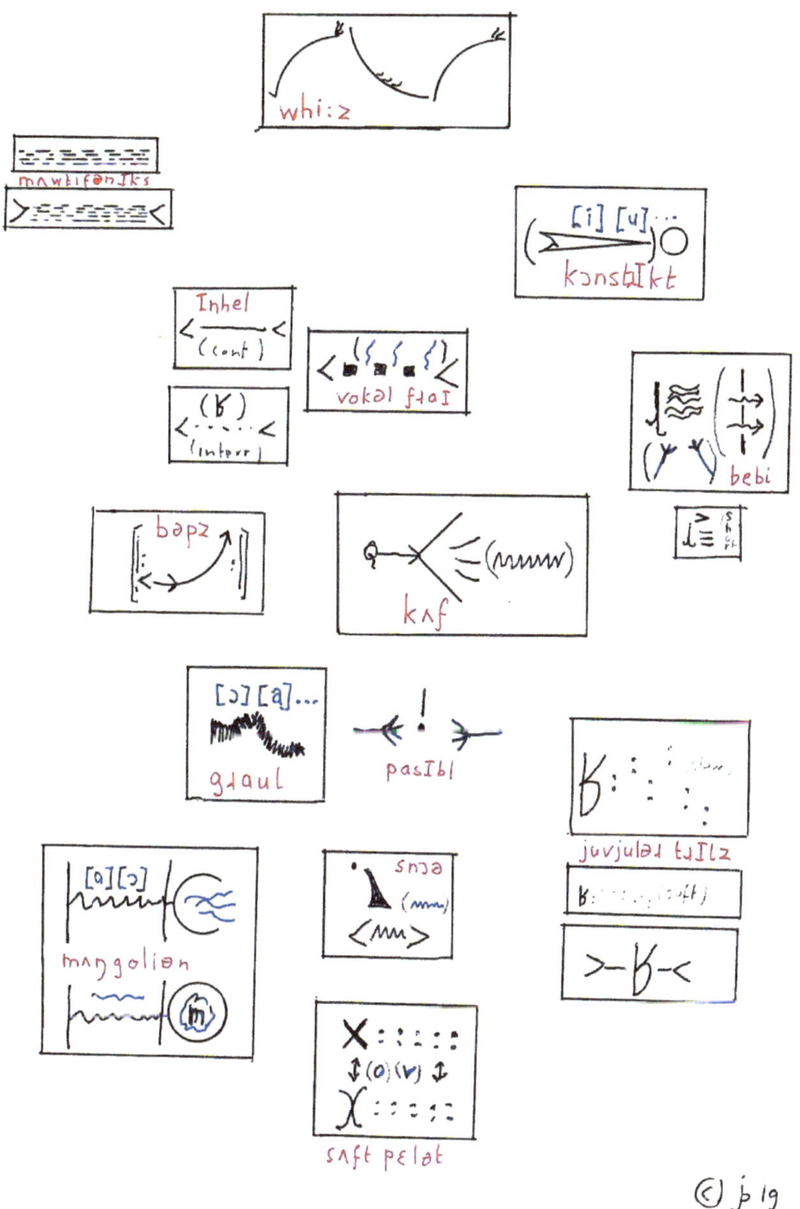

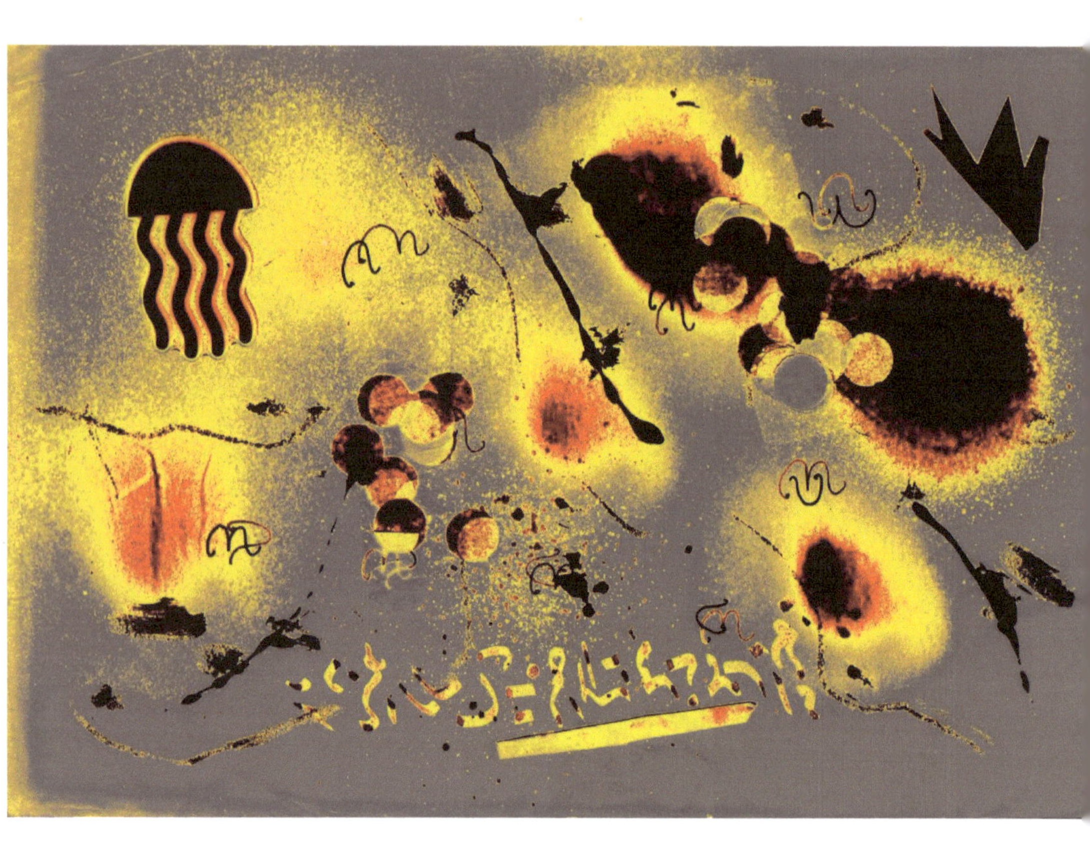

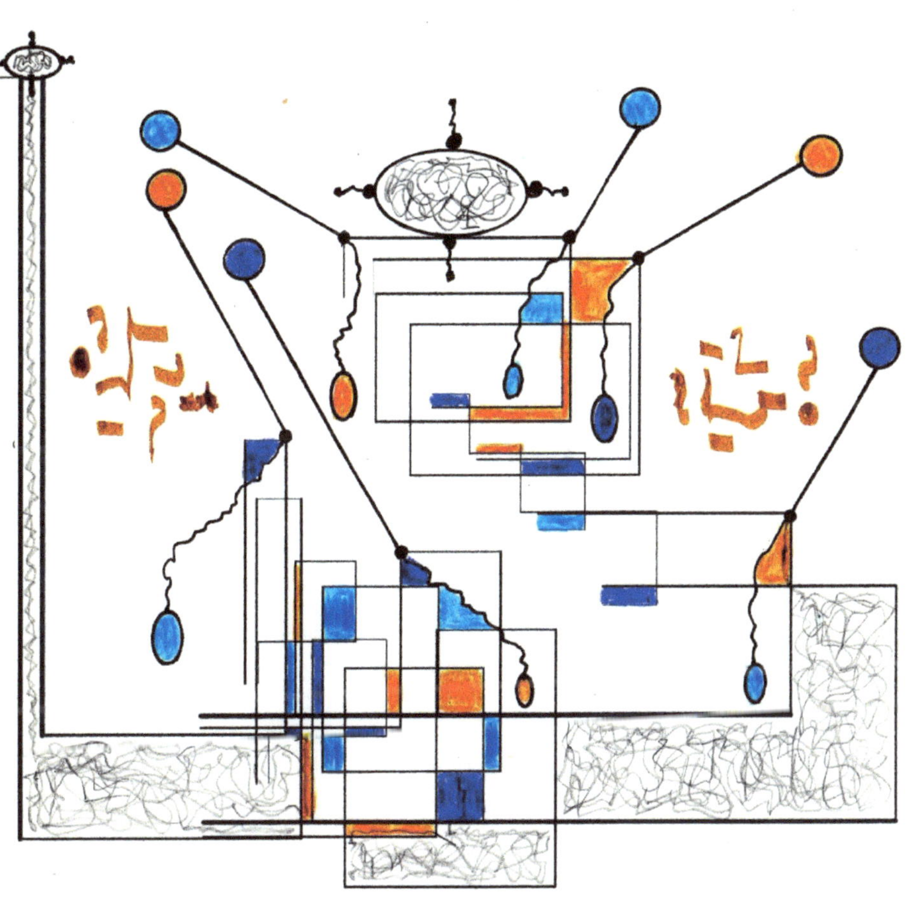

Alexander Laurence
STORY ONE: The Eleven Cousins

Gather around and allow me to tell you the story of The Eleven Cousins. Years ago, we all lived in a suburban neighborhood. All the houses looked the same. All the houses were walled off into private communities. Many of our parents worked for the same aerospace company. You could look down the street and see the same type of two or three bedroom house that continued on for what seemed like infinity. All the families were of a similar size too. Families with three brothers or three sisters were a common theme, or one of each. I endured many years of middle school with little if no deviation from this basic sameness. That all changed when I discovered the existence of The Eleven Cousins.

One fall night I went to bed and closed my eyes on the previous known world. When I woke up, I had breakfast with my family. This day seemed like many happy days which preceded it. My brother said: "It looks like somebody moved in across the street." My curiosity also brought me to the front window. I looked out and I expected to see yet another family much like ours. That didn't happen. I saw an ominous group hovered around some focal point of interest in their front yard. I will refer to this strange group as The Eleven Cousins.

The Eleven Cousins were not so much a family. They were much more like a cult. The Eleven Cousins were not old. The Eleven Cousins were not young. I may be confusing here focusing too much on qualities that they lacked. Let me describe them properly. The Eleven Cousins wore long flowing robes. The Eleven Cousins had long hair. The Eleven Cousins were all very tall and thin. They all had pale faces and long hands. I couldn't really tell if they were male or female, or which ones were the children or the parents, for at first I kept my distance, and at this point, I only viewed them from a few hundred feet distance with a long unknowing gaze.

Many families in the neighborhood had barbecues or pool parties. The Eleven Cousins never did any of these dull activities. No one had ever saw them at school or at the local supermarket. They never used cars or bicycles. As far as I knew most of their time was spent indoors. Then I discovered that three times a day, The Eleven Cousins would huddle in the front yard. They walked around as a group. I had some friends over during a pool party. The Eleven Cousins appeared on the lawn. My best friend asked: "Who are those people?" I told him that I didn't know their names. "Those are our new neighbors" I said. I could often hear noises and muttering, but I couldn't make out any words.

Months went by. The Eleven Cousins didn't conform to any human principles that we were aware of. The Eleven Cousins didn't attend church of school.

The Eleven Cousins didn't work or have jobs. The Eleven Cousins just existed like some black crows in nearby trees. I could hear them at times, but I wasn't even sure if they were speaking English. People were also aware of them but soon started to ignore them.

I spoke to my cousin who lived in another city twenty miles away. This cousin would later in life commit suicide. I told him about The Eleven Cousins.

My cousin said: "Oh yeah! I remember them!"

"Remember them?" I asked.

"Yeah. They used to lived near me. We didn't call them The Eleven Cousins though. I am not sure they are actually related to each other. We called them The Mob."

"The Mob?"

"Not like the mob, as in organized crime. More like a mob of insects. So one day, they left. They were gone. Some people told me that they died in a mass suicide in the desert. That may be a rumor."

"Yes. That story was not true."

"How do you know?"

"I am looking at them right now. They live right across the street from me where Mr. Condo used to live."

"Oh right" my cousin replied. "I will make sure that we don't visit your family any time soon."

More months passed. The Eleven Cousins started to become like some old toys that were placed in the garage and forgotten about. The Eleven Cousins were like the trees and the grass, except they didn't seem to grow or change shape. They were creepy but for some reason I didn't fear them nor have any nightmares about them. They were a living blob that existed somehow. I stopped looking for answers.

At the moment The Eleven Cousins almost became invisible to me, some other neighbors took notice of them. There was some sort of town meeting meant to address the bizarre existence of The Eleven Cousins. At this meeting, there were strict laws made that were meant to deal with The Eleven Cousins. All children had to go to school. There could not be any meetings on lawns with more than ten people. And so on. There were almost twenty new laws meant to disrupt the life of The Eleven Cousins.

A week passed and I didn't see much difference in my daily life. The Eleven Cousins ignored these laws I guessed. I don't think that they huddled on the lawn anymore. For if they did, they would be immediately arrested by the police who now were parked nearby on lookout. Instead of meeting on their lawn, they would walk around the neighborhood in a spider-like formation. This was much worse. Instead of just existing in their house, they were in everyone's eyesight. More complaints followed.

Another town meeting happened. It was more violent than the previous one. People proposed some drastic action to take place. Since most families only contained at most seven or eight members, it was then decided that no family could live in this neighborhood in a house with more than eight family members. They had a vote. A majority agreed that this was the new law. A letter was sent to The Eleven Cousins requiring them to respect this law. It was the end of winter, and they were to move out and leave on that certain date.

I was sad to see them go. I went to bed that night imagining that I had seen the last of The Eleven Cousins.

I woke up the next day and had breakfast with my family. My brother looked out the window and said "Hey everyone, it's gone!"

"It's gone?" I asked. My brother was callous at times but I always considered The Eleven Cousins as people and not a thing.

I came to the window myself and said: "Oh damn, you're right!" The house of The Eleven Cousins had disappeared overnight. It was just a flat slab of cement now. Only the foundation remained. Behind the foundation, in the back yard, was a big tent. The Eleven Cousins were still there. Now they lived in this tent and walked around the neighborhood three times a day. People again protested. There were wars going on, poverty, illness, and injustice, and all people cared about was removing The Eleven Cousins from this little town.

The Eleven Cousins continued living in the tent for a while. Unfortunately for them, that winter, and early part of year, was also the biggest rainy season of my life. The winds howled for weeks. I couldn't leave the house at times, and often the power went out, and we were all huddled in the living room, waiting for the heat to come back on. My family sat together near a small fire and waited for things to return back to normal.

Soon winter became spring, and we were on the verge of summer. I woke up one day and The Eleven Cousins were gone. They had left and packed their bags.

Many years have passed and I would never again see or hear about The Eleven Cousins again. I guess they have moved from town to town over the years. At first they were a novelty, and then later they were chased out of town. As an older man, I have traveled all over the world hoping to see some trace of The Eleven Cousins. I look forward to that day. Now looking back, years later, all I can remember about childhood was its awkwardness. With that, I conclude my story about The Eleven Cousins.

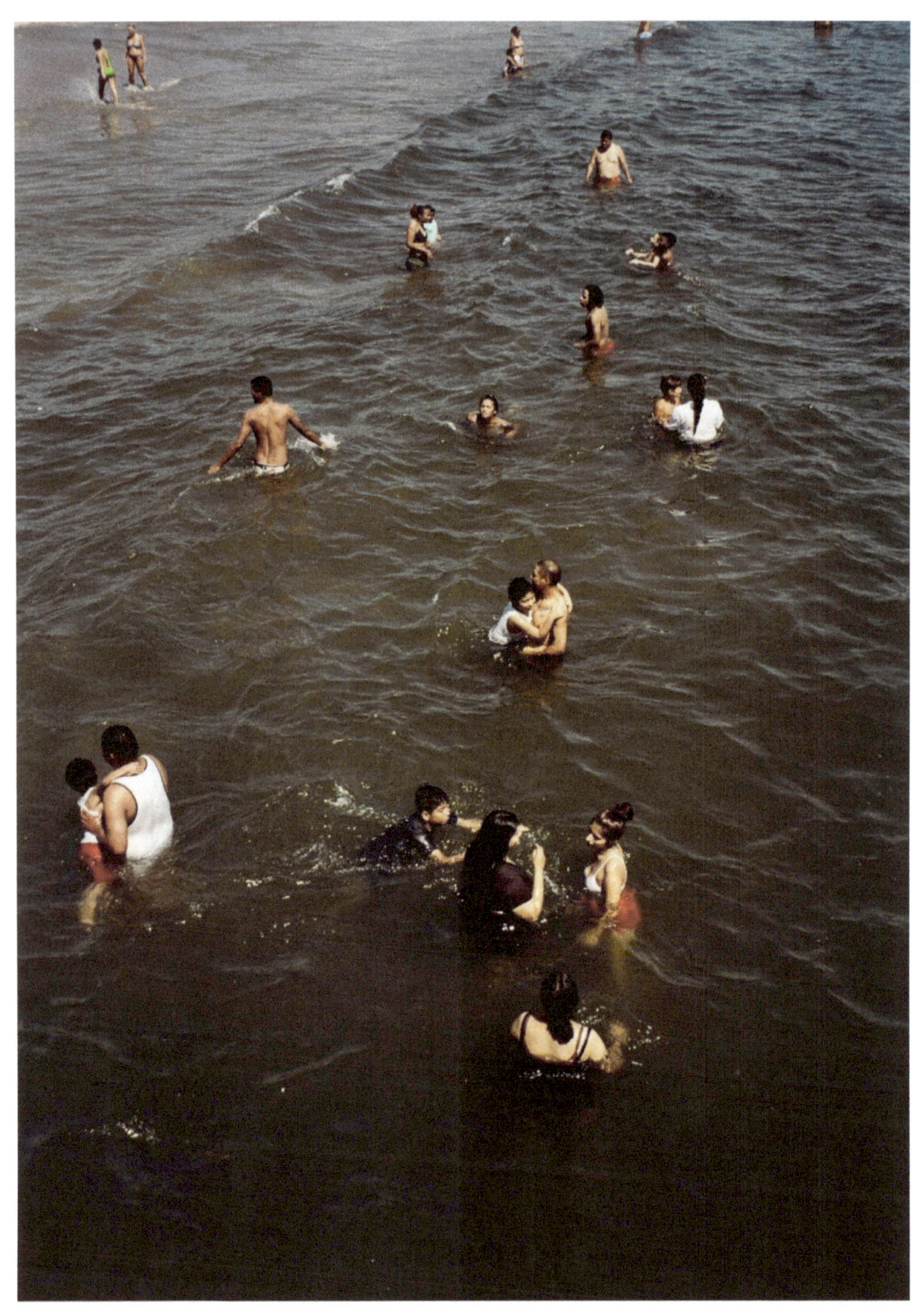

vonvivsview **TOGETHER**

Ann Pedone
Poems from "nymphe"

From: JFK

Nipple Hair [3]

Jack in the situation room with Bobby on the phone

his penis hiding somewhere between his legs

Or, maybe it is just the direct line to Khrushchev set up by State two
weeks before

He scratches it

Picks up a black pen and waving it at the phone feels all of his milk

come up from his testicles into his belly

Jackie is in the residence trying out a new box of light bulbs

the kind that always seem to have moral questions

Before he ran for the Senate he was most famous in Boston for

being the man who could get a hard-on just from someone
touching his left

elbow

Every neuron in his cock fires twice

Then he says the word Moscow and inhales all the air in the
room

the red muscles behind his eyes twitch

his lungs close wetly around the map of Cuba taped to the table

And the fish along the shores of Kennebunkport rise
to the surface

I told Jackie I have never known where to put all of my need

Later, in a night full of sticky dreams and rice
he will move his fist

to the center of

his chest, rub the wet skin around his neck

I need to stop sleeping with my mouth open
otherwise I will wake with a belly full of husbands

The body and one's sex are two parallel lines that never meet

or so said Walter Cronkite

And he rings the front desk at the Parker Hotel, says that

a certain Mr. Birch would like room 347 for Wed and
Thurs of the following

week

Rubs

his nipple hair and turns off every single last one
of the lights

White [2]

Your eggs are shit
The gynecologist
said

I looked down into
my lap
thought about

little baby
Patrick
The child John and Jackie had

lost
I cried because
I am not
used to
not being
beautiful in every
single

way

I don't know
the color of the dress
Jackie wore
when she left
the hospital that
day. But I remember it
looked
like a maternity

dress. Maybe
her
belly was still large or
she hadn't brought

a change of

clothes

When I first saw that film
I

was 9 or 10. Now

I am 52. And

I will tell you
I
think
she was
hiding
behind that dress. Because

her
heart was
rubber and
blind

When I

found out from my
doctor that
I am too old to
get
pregnant

we
were stuck
in terminal one
you

tried to finger me
when we were
in
line to buy
water and
sleeping

pills. Then we
got shitfaced and almost
missed the
flight to
JFK

My

body is

unrecognizable to me
compared with

three

years ago

In all
honesty

I have
never loved this hotel
Some-
thing about it feels
uncherished and
filled with
sweat

If you could stay
a little longer if
you didn't have to

rush
home to her I would

show you

the Jackie
clip
on my laptop

It is in black & white

Not like movies
today. These days where
everything
absolutely

every
last thing

is in color

Greek [3]

This morning all of the men
At the market
Seemed to know
One

Squeezed an eggplant
One bought a large jar of
Greek

Olives
When I picked up
A package of peppered
Salami it
Suddenly occurred to me how
Grossly

Impractical

How wildly
Unrealistic
It is to imagine
Something like language
Can
Do the job

I leave tomorrow
At 7
I will text you from the plane if there
Is
Free Wi-fi

I don't know
Maybe
I am just hormonal but
Sometimes I
Think the word desire
Really doesn't
Signify
Like it

Used to

Rhys Daly
On 3 AM With All My Former Roommates

I poltergeist a toilet tank

  Have you sent another invitation

  to the monsters knocking?

while the neon screams -

  Open at 6 AM!

God, we should have been there in the Winter!

Back when the sun was still hidden,

my nose pressing your glasses into your eyes.

  What if the bus stop angel was on to something?

I'm reminded there's always a flotilla of stimuli here

  Oscillations of blue and red,

  pulsing,

  driving tears from our eyes

behind the blast shield of fatigue

  Whose hand is on our neck?

as I lock into the carpet.

Toes curling, carving lines in the shag

like in the bedsheets of my first boyfriend in college.

  Someone is leaving out the back door!

The coin operated breathalyzer

gnashes its teeth at me.

I gnash back

Gnash.

I imagine my glare off a fencepost.

  Gnash.

I press my tongue against it.

Gnash.

I prowl in the domesticity,
the rhythmic glugging of the sink,
almost desirable when I'm sober.

You have a common fantasy when you drink
  I'm bashing in the head of my brother-in-law

  with a cellphone

  while he laughs.
Horrid.
  I'm a bone degreaser

  a heretical midge with a cellphone-
and a dream
to fill the ridges in the wood pile
behind the house.
  Achievement works its way to the quick.

  I am painfully effervescent.

  The fire roars-
Higher!

I bend over backwards,
draining into the ceiling until I'm grey.
  Drink tomorrow's headache slowly

  it will be like vomiting into a stranger's toilet.

  Blink.

Blink red with me, babies,
blink red as the refrigerator creaks.

Rhys Daly

Rhys Daly
Guilt

Do not look at the moon. Don't, that's what they say. She is shining. Can you believe it? So full of moonshine and screaming. So full. Imagine. Imagine you're looking at the moon, have you seen her (is she her?) in your imagination. The crescent of crescents descending in your imagination. The night in your head was never so full of moon. It was full of cowboys and lip-locked cliques that reminded you of high school. Cruel and truly cowboy filled.

It's cool out, ain't it? That's how they said it, ain't it?

I think, I truly think the cowboys sleep at night so they do not have to look at the moon, that inverse of a moth. A furry night-thing that rests on cowboys' brows when they are tired of looking at the moon they have not seen.

I can't believe the moths are full of moonshine. I'm afraid I've closed my eyes again. I'm afraid I've closed my eyes again, moths. I'm afraid to look at the moon. The moon may look back. What if the moon is beautiful? What if the moon looks like my mother? What if the moon is a man? What if the moon is a man like the cowboy who couldn't write, but could draw beautiful things like crows erupting into branches that snatch the life from my eyes and cram it into my chest so full of a bird with sticks for a head? The moon may be full of sticks! Full of sticks and a flag. Toothpicks. The moon is full of toothpicks, this is where we get toothpicks from, you see? Imagine saving the rainforest only to kill the moon by harvesting all those toothpicks. Imagine how many exotic moths may be saved by killing the moon.

It would make me so happy to kill the moon to save the moths even though I despise moths and love the moon. I'm so afraid of moths, what if their wings are delicate and will wilt if I touch them? Wings that can sit through a storm, but at my fingertips would melt like ice and I would have icy moth blood on my hands. Mothblood, mothblood, imagine all the mothblood that will be saved by killing the moon!

But if I look at the moon and the moon is not toothpicks, I'd be disappointed as I wade through the littering mothwings. Is it the moon's fault that she is not made of toothpicks?

Yes, she. The moon is a woman covered in the scales of moth wings and I am looking at her face.

I am not the moon, but still she is beautiful.

Rhys Daly
Road Trip Benediction

There's the soft serve ice cream shop

the beacon of home,

      elevated to a cowlick on a seraphim's crown

now abandoned.

There is a sketch of myself as a child on the bench

      hazy but specific,

with eraser crumbs for the mole on my left shoulder.

You,

sketch, on those benches!

Rejoice!

You will introduce yourself by your initials

to the owner of the ocean in twelve years.

You will part your hair intentionally

      covet life

and disappear from this puddle to live in an oyster penthouse.

You will chew on sand and raw lentils,

clap your hands raw and breathe in all the putrid air,

relishing guiltlessly.

So rotten to the core you will be

      but so violently unmistakable

that crowd of angels will lose themselves

in hopes of glimpsing

your oil slick hair.

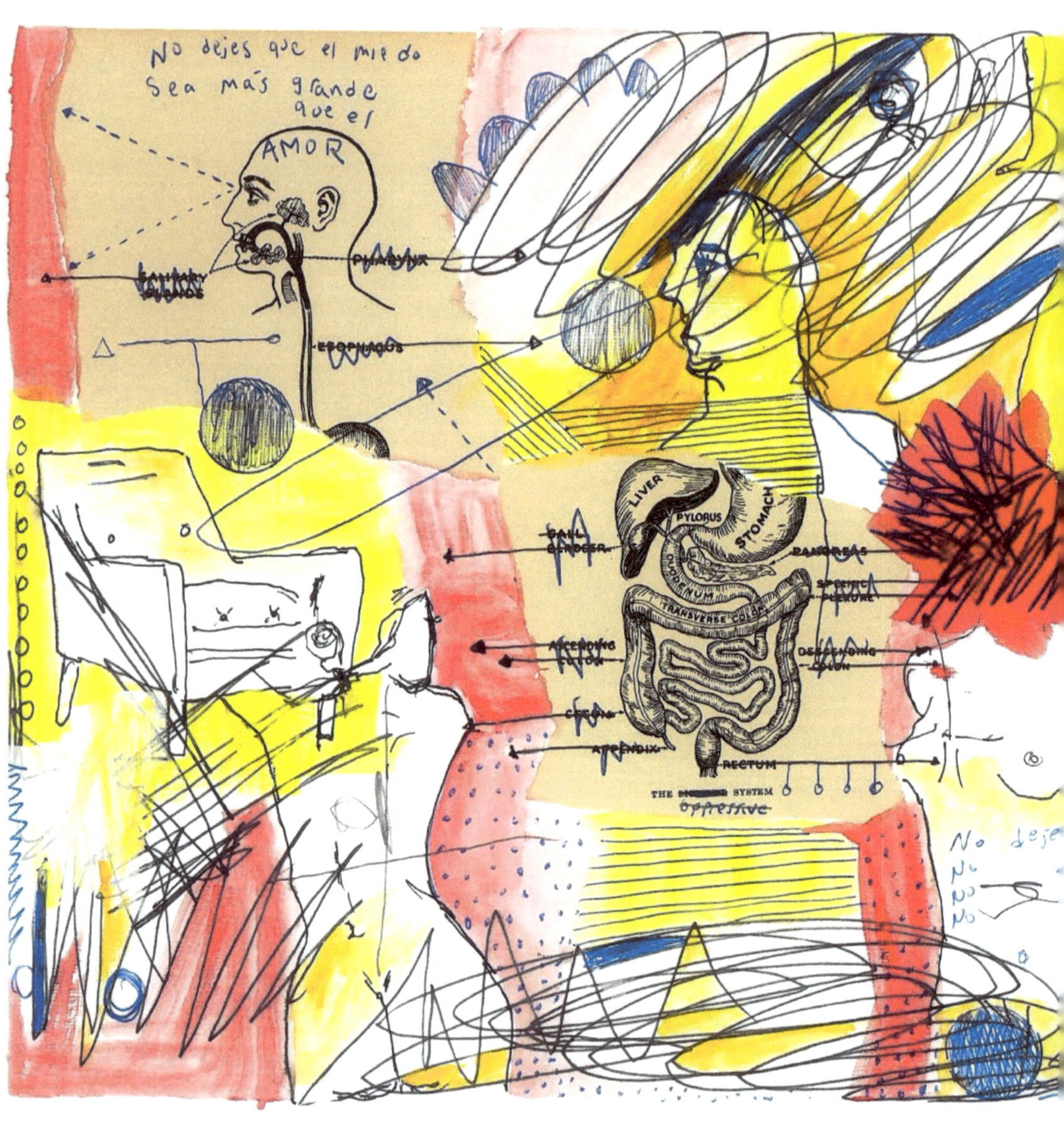

Octavio Quinatnilla **Untitled**

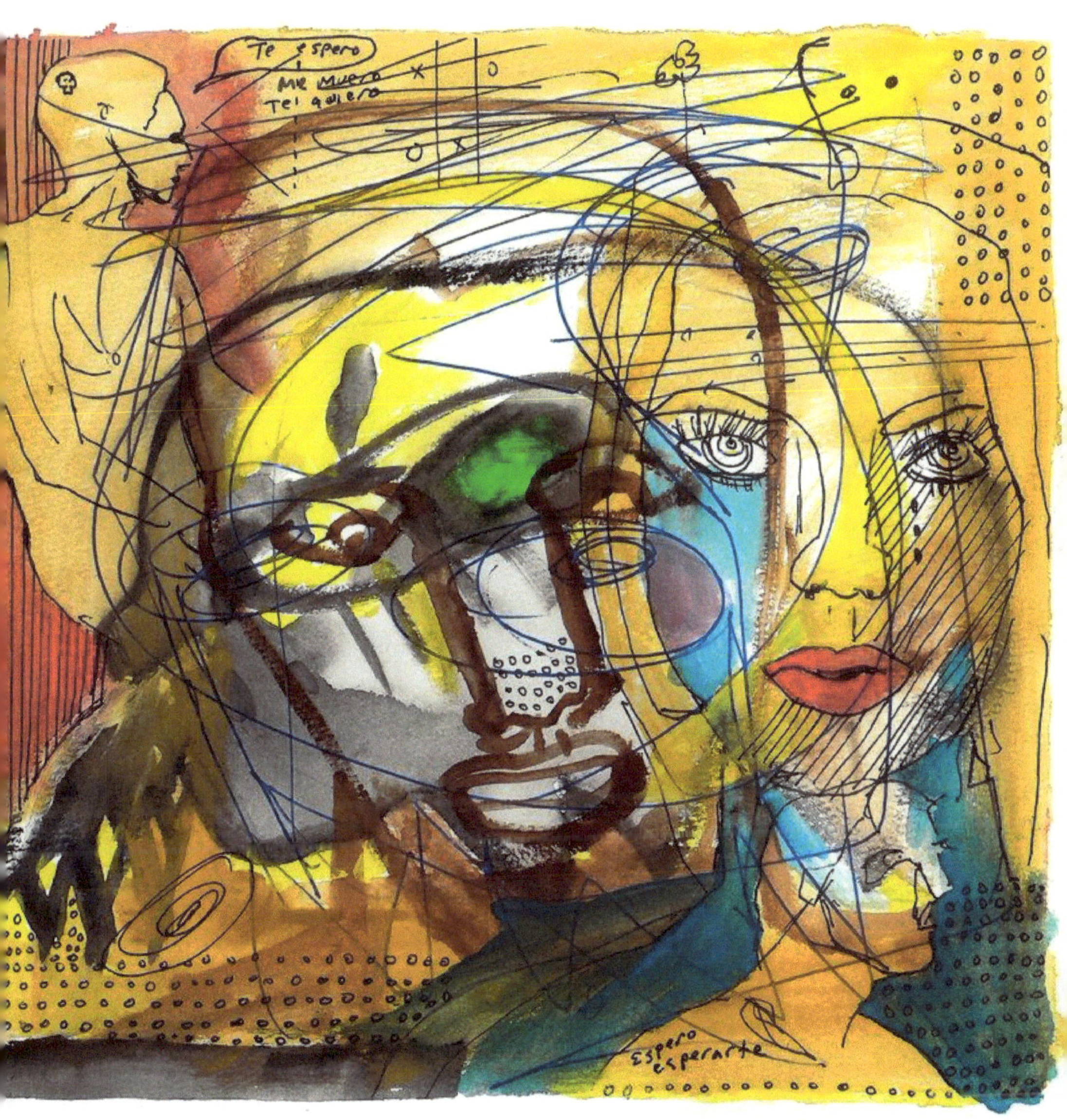

Octavio Quinatnilla **Pasaporte 43**

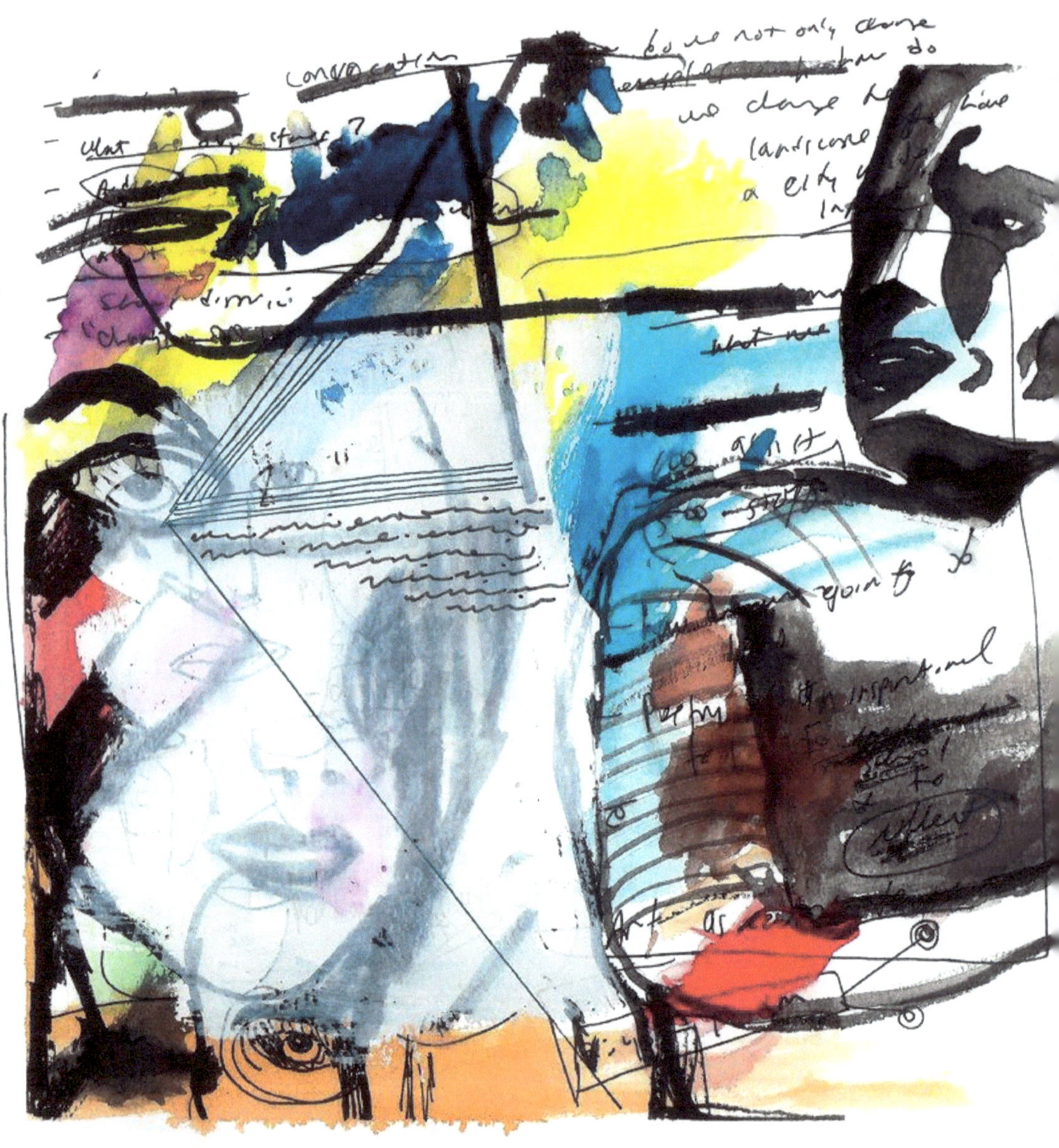

Octavio Quinatnilla **Pasaporte 40**

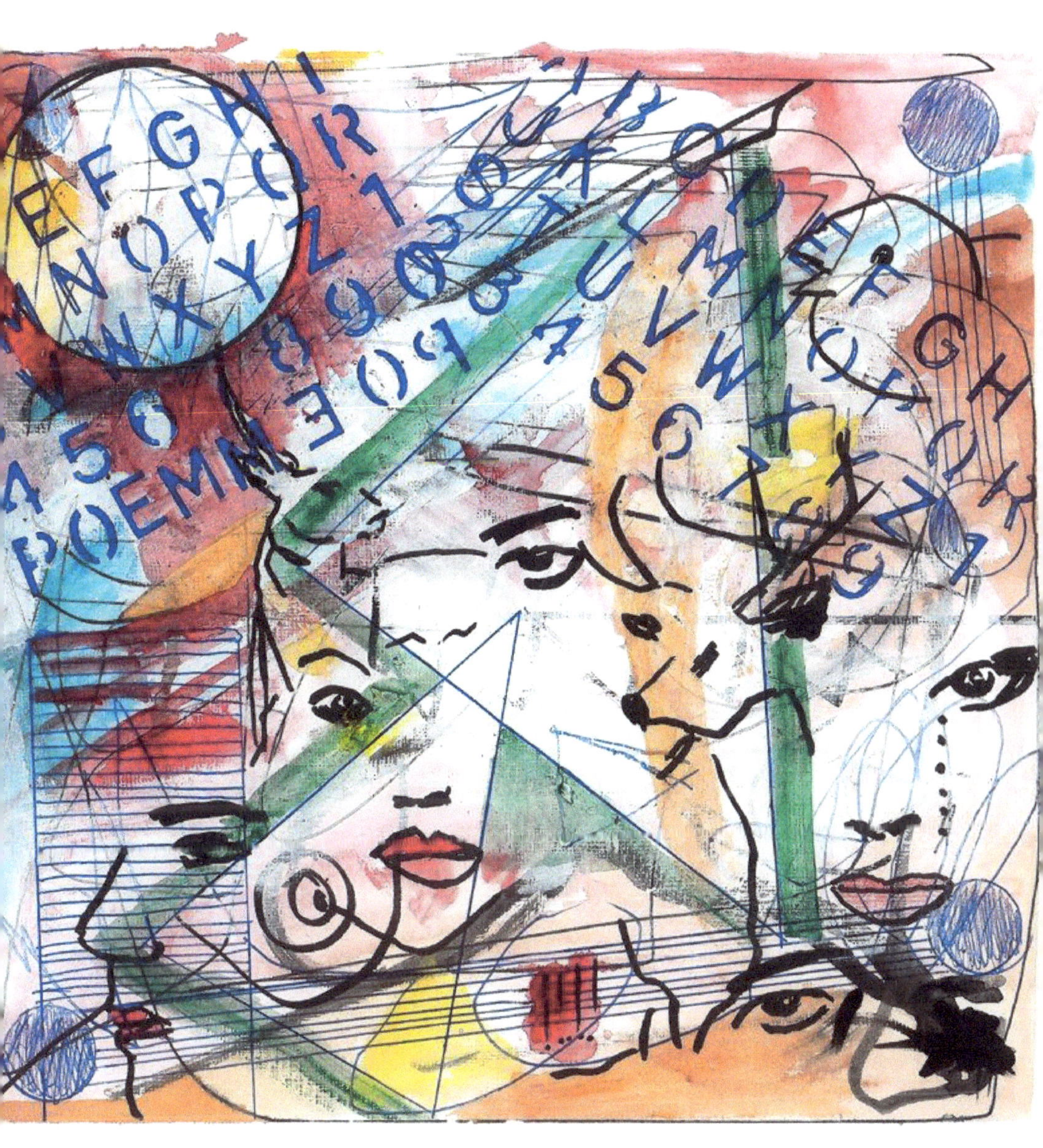

Octavio Quinatnilla **Pasaporte 15**

Lily Lavender Wolf
Golden Teacher

once there was a holy mushroom
lived in my daddy's closet for five years

i prayed, for music, for pollen, for orgasms everlasting
my wishes were granted in kisses from angels
all the poetry i could dream up
colorful and worldly

i prayed, for endless nights, for visions of sweet seraphim

this
awesome agaric
my lovely golden teacher
cosmetic universe all in a single blue spore
the notes of twilight electric held in holy lesson
i danced miasmic moonlight away

once there was a land where faeries held hands,
rubbed clitori
spore sprites peacefully nocturne in love in life

and a sweet sweet eighth of eros
the holiest cap of all

Karen Falcone Krieger

Doing the Work, Happy with the Imagery

Student Survey MTV (dream, 1/6/20)   Prof. Falcone

What is your name?
looking at stars
What do you prefer to be called? (Nickname)
noticing my eyes
adjust as the neighbors
If I need to reach you quickly, how do you prefer to be contacted? Cell phone,
turn the lights
text, personal email, OW email, home phone? Please provide:

The neighbor is you
up in the attic
What is your home town or high school?
looking for the switch
the aperture opens
Did you take remedial or ESL classes in the past? Which? For how long?
and I see shooting stars

Are you a transfer student? From what college?
 You return with your
Are you repeating this class? For what reason?
 I know the song before
How fast can it go?   Second time?   Third time?
 from the opening note
Are you a student with a disability? Have you registered with OSSD?
 we hear that
Do you work? How many hours per week? Where?
 the first year of MTV?

Where do you live? (On campus, at home, etc.)
 Your little sister Jenny
is there. I give her
Who do you live with? Do you have family responsibilities? (childcare, etc.)
a blazer for her
job interview tomorrow
How do you get to college? Drive, bus, get rides, etc.
 Who *are* you? she asks
Major? Job to get? Future Plans?
me this blazer and
Is there anything else you would like me to know about you? Feel free to write on
me by asking this page. (I love to write. I hate to read out loud in class. I need to
earn a B, etc.)
I look at you
and say
I chose him and
he chose me.

"Well, while I'm here I'll
do the work –
and what's the Work?
To ease the pain of living.
Everything else, drunken
dumbshow."
-Allen Ginsberg,

… I finally stopped
twenty years an adjunct, freshman comp
and then were all these other things
like Sunday and Tuesday.
Saw a fox in Massachusetts
a great blue heron when we got home
Saw the new moon's shining slice
and a planet in the west.
doing its work.
Saturday morning
Lee and I drive up to Mass.
stop at the store   wait on a line   buy legal grass.
Pick up Ross.
It's Chinese New Year,
Year of the Rat
its grey   we find
a table at the Chinese
buffet
looks a little rugged   at 2:30.
The chef makes us fresh
chicken and broccoli
We hear him   working the wok.
Happy New Year!
He says bringing out the tray.

Saturday afternoon at Walmart
Brockton, Mass
for the guys to buy swim trunks,
the announcement, repeatedly:
"Joan Baez, please come to the service desk."
I find a jar of honey from Virginia.
"Joan Baez, please come to the service desk."

At the Hampton Inn   the indoor pool
              is full of sloshing kids.
I don't undress.
         The guys go down to look at it.
                "Raindrops Keep Falling on My Head"
                             is playing in the elevator.
         Ross shaves in our hotel room.
                No razors are allowed at his house.
I ask if he cleaned up the sink   he says yes
              good work I say.
         Later I see the new white bar
                of hotel soap   covered with black hairs.
                His face looks better, though.

         Saturday night in the rain
                     the three of us at Dave and Busters.
         I drank Long Island Iced Teas
                                        too fast
         when out of plays of skee ball
                go looking for Lee and Ross
for hours
         walking in circles   *and hours*
                bells and lights and drunk parents
                        and young kids dashing.
         When I find them   I am told
                only 8 minutes have passed.
Passing out on the work.
                Happy with the imagery.

         On the way home Sunday
                     we stopped and hiked
                            somewhere in Connecticut.
We could look across the Sound
                                    and see our town,
                but still had a long way to drive.
         The sun came out
                     wind ripped the ridge.
When I stepped to the edge
                                        the fox
                moved from the unseen ledge
              beneath us
       where he was warming himself.
                     It was an old fox and he trotted
       'til he was out of sight   through the winter forest.

At home I thought   it was a spider
                                                   trying to get inside.
                  It was only bird
                        poop on the window
                                      this cold Sunday night.

                  Tuesdays I see my therapist Sandy.
Afterward   I often eat carbs and shop
Sometimes   I drink too much or nap.
                  I wanted to talk about shame.
                        It seems to keep coming up.
                              She is quick to seize on it.
Today it is two brioche rolls
                      from the old school bakery   with butter.

                  Later I'm printing on the backs
                            of all my old teaching handouts:
            syllabi, surveys, assessments,
                            assignments   *violence.*
I'm printing new stuff on the back:
                      dreams, notes, a book review, a palimpsest,
            an article a listicle a long ass essay.
I make the back the front
                            back once blank now faces forward.
                  I do this work in haste   and make mistakes
                      against mortality and shame
                                        happy
                        with the imagery.
Let's just say   doing the work
                        is the impulse to poetry.

Elizabeth Poreba
Beginning At the East River,

where Cuban ships sat low in the water
with the weight of the stuff

DOMINO
upward slanting signature

yellow bag of the purveyor
anonymous master

dedicated to sweetening the lives of countless
fish perhaps gathered to savor what stevedores lost

My attention flags, eyes of the mind
fixed on the sign, soon to be up again

by the condominiums
taking the "cool factor" to a new level

A ferry now distracts, two bikers chatter,
one jogger lifts his knees so prettily

Glass homes stacked flat
What keeps the waters back?

Sweet that meets no need, appetite
cheaply appeased. heaping teaspoon

to the cup, and again, never enough
Cravings that have carved the skyline

with the fall from snowy chutes,
an arrangement seeming so absolute —

A police boat speeds by, chin up
The river heaves, spoons swirling in cups.

Elizabeth Poreba
A Kind of Honey

found in cane, white as gum,
that crunches between the teeth[1]

When crystalized, easy
to commodify

Hispaniola the first plantation
Get your land, get your cane,

get your people
trade in a triangle, neat visual:

from Africa, go west,
make molasses, take it north,

and sail rum back, a map
of orderly industry

with devotion's visage, we
sugar o'er the devil himself[2]

---

[1] Pliny the Elder writes: 'Sugar is made in Arabia as well, but Indian sugar is better. It is a kind of honey found in cane, white as gum, and it crunches between the teeth. It comes in lumps the size of a hazelnut. Sugar is used only for medical purposes.'

[2] Hamlet, Act 3, Scene 1. Polonius to Ophelia

Elizabeth Poreba
Nice,

you must surround yourself with nice things
she said, my mother at coffee,

center of the table, her vase of silver spoons, a bouquet
of finials where flowers should be

I chose one to stir, then carefully propped
for her to polish when she washed up

One spoon ribbed like a scallop shell
wide as a smile, rugged to the lips

never meant to touch, for scooping only
from bowl to cup (a wet spoon leaves lumps)

Flowered neck, easily tarnished,
requires diligence

and is rough to soft fingers
Nice she said, meaning objects

of small utility
requiring much activity ,

Elizabeth Poreba
Even now,

what I most often want
is the long ago, sweet ,withheld

then proffered, dangled to be earned
or to keep me still, small packet

in many colors, or mother making fudge
waiting for it to cool soft at first

Such appetite,
the *usurper of true hunger*

according to Ramana Maharihi[3]
via Paul Brunton[4], Victorian essayist

who donned the guru
like a smoking jacket,

made from silk that was also
from other parts, so many imports.

Proverbs

advises those given to appetite,
Put a knife in thy throat[5]

but we say, rev it up, it's the engine
powering boats sent out

to every country, exchanging
their goods for our cargoes of vacancy

---

[3] https://www.sriramanamaharshi.org/

[4] Paul Brunton is the pen name of Raphael Hurst (21 October 1898 – 27 July 1981), a British author of spiritual books. He is best known as one of the early popularizers of Neo-Hindu spiritualism in western esotericism, notably via his bestselling A Search in Secret India (1934)

[5] Proverbs 23:2

Vicki Austin
Sugar Burns

Toes snagged in the archway of your cotton-candy avarice,
bile and sweets spurt the ground, covering my spindly limbs in
a saccharine homage to the thunder labeled Niagara Falls *thirst*.
You sanctioned the glass entrance, shattering pocket-sized crimson shards of
my resolve.
"Watch it, Pussy." Oily breath puckered my skin.
Shiny silver tables cut the room.
Tables as a warm knife in butter.
Tables as legs spread before sex.
"Fuck You," you snarled
over your yellow Dixie-plate-sun solar system.
The fruit flies extinguished themselves within cracks and crevices.
We the benevolent ones?
Her fat flesh hanging from that rip with love spewing around the tangled
threads.
You laughed a purple, mottled, writhing, nakedness.
She smacked your head against the chalkboard *I loved pounding erasers against the
brick wall* as words bulged from your eyes.
You didn't even have to try to feel my breast.
I grabbed that cage and cradled It carefully home.
Over mountains and speed bumps, flaming neighborhoods and barbed wire.
Gorged on Thin Mints.
Freed It.
Soothed It.
Sang to It.
Covered It in dirt.
Crybaby, you accused.
Maybe so. I mused, licking my chapped lips.

Kimberly Jae
Domestic Violence Respectability Politics

Name: I█████████████████ age 10)

<u>CCSS.ELA-LITERACY.RI.6.8</u>
Trace and evaluate the argument and specific claims in a text, distinguishing claims that are supported by reasons and evidence from claims that are not.

Directions: As you read the claim below, consider how the author uses the,
- Evidence to support his/her claim
- Reasoning to develop his/her claim
- The pictures to persuade the reader to believe his/her claim

Write an essay in response to the author's claim. Use BCR (brief constructed response) format to agree or disagree with the author's claim. Explain your response. You will not lose points for spelling.

Claim: <u>They deserved it.</u>

Evidence: <u>Look at them.</u>

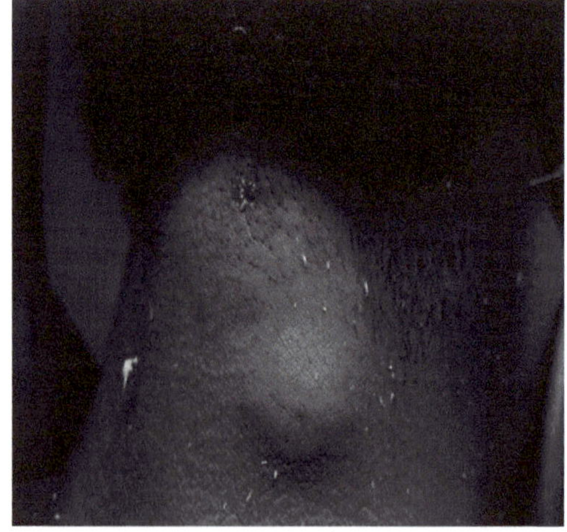

Physical Abuse

Rape/Sexual Abuse

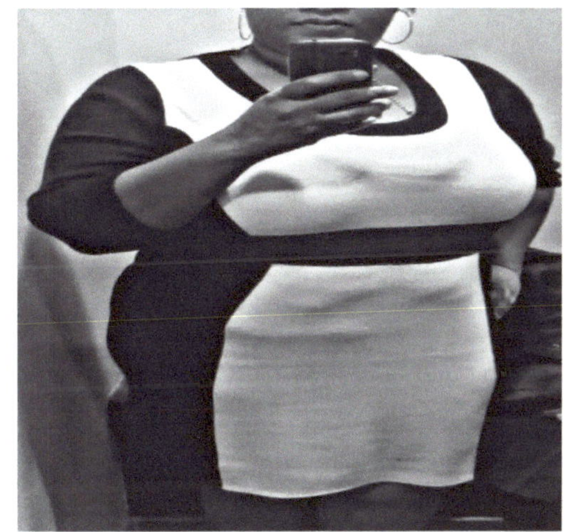

Emotional/ Financial Abuse

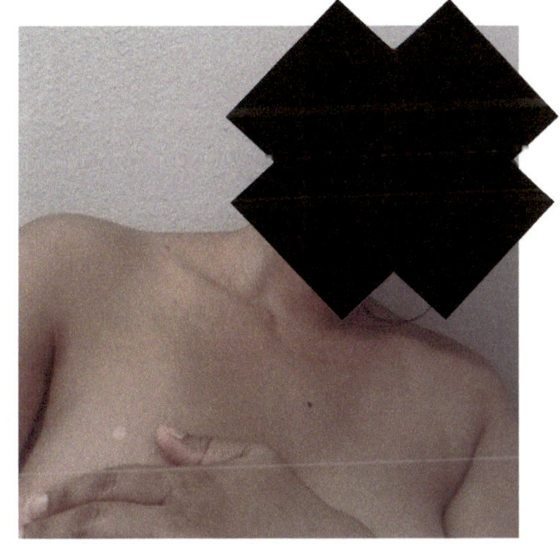

When I say she disserved it
I mean
She stupid
Nappy headed gurls are bad
Disserve to be hit
My momma say
Uh little jealous
Uh little 'citement
Uh man hits you
'cause he love you
He teach you to do right
He be paying bills
You gotta be good
Gotta show him you uh good gurl
The Bible say
Women gotta move in silence
Why she putting they bizness in the street?

Don't nobody rape fat gurls
She lyin'
Don't nobody want fat gurls
He could git anybody
Why he want to rape hur?

She uh gold digger
She wont money and
Don't disserve it
She ain't got no clothes on
She baldheaded
She look like uh boy
She uh hoe
She disserve to be called uh hoe
Why a man wanna give hur his money?

Gurls that git abused
is pretty white gurls
who be virgins and
beleive in Jesus and
go to church and
have mommas and daddies that are married and
live in houses together

not gurls that look like me.

Black gurls ain't allowed to be
Victims

And if he did
Jesus say forgive
The Bible say
Women gotta submit

Ain't this submitting?

CONTRIBUTORS

Vicki Austin's work has been featured on the Erma Bombeck Writers' Workshop blog, included in the online journals Projected Letters and Wraparound South and printed in The Walls Between Us: Essays in Search of Truth, a Juncture publication.

Jaap Blonk (born 1953 in Woerden, Netherlands) is a self-taught composer, performer and poet. His unfinished studies in mathematics and musicology mainly created a penchant for activities in a Dada vein, as did several unsuccessful jobs in offices and other well-organized systems. In the late 1970s he took up saxophone and started to compose music. A few years later he discovered his potential as a vocal performer, at first in reciting poetry and later on in improvisations and his own compositions.From around the year 1995 on Blonk started work with electronics, at first using samples of his own voice, then extending the field to include pure sound synthesis as well. He took a year off of performing in 2006. His renewed interest in mathematics made him start a research of the possibilities of algorithmic composition for the creation of music, visual animation and poetry. As a vocalist, Jaap Blonk is unique for his powerful stage presence and keen grasp of structure, even in free improvisation. He has performed around the world, on all continents. With the use of live electronics, and sometimes projection of visuals, the scope and range of his concerts has acquired a considerable extension. Blonk's recorded / published output comprises some 60 titles: CDs, vinyl, books and cassettes. From his sound poetry scores he developed an independent body of visual work, which has been exhibited and collected in books. See tofuink.com to experience Jaap's brilliant recordings.

Rhys Daly is a queer Asian-American Seattle writer and actor who wishes he lived even closer to the ocean. His work explores discomfort, uncertainty, identity, acceptance, and the wonder in the mundane. When he's not hunched over a coffee table furiously memorizing lines or scribbling up poems, he can be found walking moodily down a city street looking for his next bit of inspiration. Other works can be found in Rigorous Magazine and Short Vine Journal as Cyan, and Cathexis Northwest Press as himself. His debut poetry collection *Shedding* is available through Unsolicited Press.

Jasper Glen is from Vancouver, Canada. He holds a BA in Philosophy and a JD. His poems appear or are forthcoming tn *Posit, Streetlight Magazine, fauxmoir, NiftyLit, Pinky Thinker Press, The Ekphrastic Review, The Antonym,* and *Island Writer Magazine.*

Genoveva Galarza Heredero's visual art is heavily inspired by ecology, speculative fiction, and human anxieties and dreams.

Harvey Humphrey (they/them) is trying to be some kind of activist-academic (they want to try to change the world through language). They are a queer, trans, non-binary disabled person living in Glasgow. They have a PhD in sociology on trans and intersex activism. Their academic work and their poems explore the everyday, relationships and bodies (specifically relating to queer, trans and disability experiences). Their favourite food is ice cream. Previously published: *Powders Press, Snowflake Magazine, Gamut Mag.* Twitter: @rharveyhumphrey

Jones Irwin teaches Philosophy and Education in Dublin, Republic of Ireland. His vision is of a postmodern existentialist, with a dash of noir mixed in with a progressivist ethic. He has been featured before in Tofu Ink.

Karin Falcone Krieger is a writer, visual artist, gardener, advocate and chef. Her writing in many genres has recently been published in *Tupelo Quarterly, Tofu Ink, Able News, Contingent Magazine, BlazeVOX, LITPUB, The Laurel Review, The Literary Review, Newsday* and other publications. She published the pop-up zine *artICHOKE.* She holds an MFA from The Jack Kerouac School of Disembodied Poetics at Naropa University. She taught freshman composition as an adjunct instructor at several New York area colleges from 1999-2019 and was involved in the organized labor movement supporting contingent faculty. She is an adult adoptee of the baby-scoop era who has been reunited with her family of origin. These and other projects can be seen at www.karinfalconekrieger.com

Brian L. Jacobs is a poet and editor of Tofu Ink Arts Press. Brian grew up in Southern California and has been teaching GATE English and Humanities for thirty one years in both K-12 and college settings. He lives in Pasadena and has been married for 17 years to Thye, a Professor of Nursing and a Nurse Practitioner. Both Thye and Brian are currently PhD candidates and will finish this year. Brian was the assistant to the Poet's Allen Ginsberg and Julie Patton while studying at Naropa. During this time he also on a peace pilgrimage with Buddhist monks commemorating WWII walking through Europe, the Middle East and India. Brian is also a three time Fulbright Scholar, which has allowed him to study in Brazil, where he studied its water issues; China, where he studied its vast 10,000 year history; and Japan, spending time to participate in a case study in one of its small towns near the Japanese Alps. He had also earned a National Endowment of Humanities grant to China, studying its philosophies and histories, a Fund For Teachers grant visiting South Africa, Swaziland and Lesotho, plus earning other various grants that have taken him to places all over in the United States. He also taught teachers at a university in Fuzhou, China for five summers under grants from SABEH. Subsequently he has earned an Earthwatch grant to the rainforest of Ecuador, to study climate change and caterpillars and he recently earned another Earthwatch Senior Fellow Grant to teach teachers in Acadia, Maine studying climate change and crabs. Brian has been to 120 countries and had visited all 50 states, practices

Yoga and is a proud vegan. Brian's poetry has been published in several publications including, *Wet Grain, Shiela-Na-Gig, the Crank, The South Florida Florida Poetry Journal, Progenitor Art and Literary Journal, GRIFFEL, Foxtail, Rip Rap, The Bangalore Review, Sunspot Lit, Anthropod, Pa'Lante, Dark Moon Lilith Press, Black Tape Press, Genre, Inky Blue/Celery, Red Dancefloor Press, Entelechy, 1844 Pine Street, Pasta Poetics, Trouble and Praxis.*

Kimberly Jae is an award-winning Slam poet and educator, who is disabled Kimberly is the winner of this years *2022 Tofu Ink Arts Press Reza Abdoh Poetry Prize.* In 2018, she became the 2018 Grand Slam Champion of Steel City Slam, BOSS Slam Queen of Steel Slam Champion, Steel City Slam IWPS Rep, and Womxn Slam Champion, going on to rank among the top 30 slam poets in the world by Poetry Slam International. In 2019, she won slams in the US and Canada, making finals for in the US and Canada as well as winning *Hot Damn, It's a Queer Slam.* Before she could compete, she survived a stroke. The condition that led to the stroke caused disability as well as a language-based disability called Aphasia, which affects her ability to read, write, speak and comprehend language. Since the stroke, she received the 2020 Zooglossia Fellowship, 2021 Langston Huges Fellowship, as well as winning a number of slams making it to finals and nationals in multiple countries. Kimberly Jae's poems and performances have been published domestically, internationally, and online including the Poetry Coalition's *One Poem: A Protest Reading in Support of Black Lives* (online), *Alt Minds Literary Magazine* (Canada), *Hawai'i Review* (US) and anthologies including, *In the Shadow of the Mic: Three Decades of Slam Poetry in Pittsburgh.* Her full-length manuscript, *Baptism*, was shortlisted for the 2021 Sexton Prize.

Alexander Laurence was born in Los Angeles. He attended CSULB and San Francisco Art Institute. He has contributed to the books The Hipster Handbook (2004), Reefer Movie Madness (2010), Degenerative Prose (1995), and books about the history of Grove Press. He is also the author of a book of short stories: Five Fingers Make A Fist (2007). He has recently written a book of poems The New Spain. He presently works as a tour manager and has traveled the world with indie bands. He is the founder of the website The Portable Infinite, and has a weekly internet radio show New Noise of Radio KAJW.

Jon Lawrence currently teaches high school English and Creative Writing in his hometown of Bethlehem, Pennsylvania. He has an MFA in Creative Writing from the Maslow Family Graduate Program in Creative Writing at Wilkes University. His poetry reviews and poetry have been published or are forthcoming from *Newfound* and *American Writers Review.* Chat with him on Twitter @JonLawrence1116

Mario Loprete I live in a world that I shape at my liking. I do this through virtual, pictorial, and sculptural movements, transferring my experiences and photographing reality through my mind's filters. I have refined this process through years of research and experimentation. Painting for me is my first love. An important, pure love. Creating a painting, starting from the spasmodic research of a concept with which I want to transmit my message this is the foundation of painting for me. The sculpture is my lover, my artistic betrayal to the painting that voluptuous and sensual lover that inspires different emotions which strike prohibited chords. This new series of concrete sculptures has been giving me more personal and professional satisfaction recently. How was it born? It was the result of an important investigation of my own work. I was looking for that special something I felt was missing.Looking back at my work over the past ten years, I understood that there was a certain semantic and semiotic logic "spoken" by my images, but the right support to valorize their message was not there. The reinforced cement, the concrete, was created two thousand years ago by the Romans. It tells a millennia-old story, one full of amphitheaters, bridges and roads that have conquered the ancient and modern world. Now, concrete is a synonym of modernity. Everywhere you go, you find a concrete wall: there's the modern man in there. From Sydney to Vancouver, Oslo to Pretoria, this reinforced cement is present, and it is this presence which supports writers and enables them to express themselves. The artistic question was an obvious one for me: if man brought art on the streets in order to make it accessible to everyone, why not bring the urban to galleries and museums? With respect to my painting process, when a painting has completely dried off, I brush it with a particular substance that not only manages to unite every color and shade, but also gives my artwork the shininess and lucidity of a poster (like the ones we've all had hanging on our walls). For my concrete sculptures, I use my personal clothing. Through my artistic process in which I use plaster, resin and cement, I transform these articles of clothing into artworks to hang. The intended effect is that my DNA and my memory remain inside the concrete, so that the person who looks at these sculptures is transformed into a type of postmodern archeologist, studying my work as urban artefacts. I like to think that those who look at my sculptures created in 2020 will be able to perceive the anguish, the vulnerability, the fear that each of us has felt in front of a planetary problem that was covid 19... under a layer of cement there are my clothes with which I lived this nefarious period. Clothes that survived covid 19, very similar to what survived after the 2,000- year-old catastrophic eruption of Pompeii, capable of recounting man's inability to face the tragedy of broken lives and destroyed economies.

Cory Massaro writes speculative poetry, fiction, and nonfiction about Luddism and the biopolitics of software.

Ann Pedone is the author of *The Medea Notebooks* (spring, 2023 Etruscan Press), and *The Italian Professor's Wife* (2022, Press 53), as well as the chapbooks *The Bird Happened, perhaps there is a sky we don't know: a re-imagining of sappho,*

Everywhere You Put Your Mouth, Sea [break], and *DREAM/WORK*. Her work has recently appeared in *The American Journal of Poetry, Chicago Quarterly Review, The Louisville Review,* and *New York Quarterly.* She has been nominated for Best of the Net, and has appeared as Best American Poetry's "Pick of the Week."

Elizabeth Poreba is a retired New York City high school English teacher. Her work has appeared in the Southern Poetry Review, the Journal of Feminist Studies in Religion, and Common-weal, among other print and online publications.
She has published two poetry collections, Vexed and Self Help: A Guide for the Retiring and two chapbooks, The Family Calling and New Lebanon.Her work can also be found in This Full Green Hour, an anthology published by the One O'Clock Poets.

Octavio Quintanilla is the author of the poetry collection, *If I Go Missing* (Slough Press, 2014) and served as the 2018-2020 Poet Laureate of San Antonio, TX. His poetry, fiction, translations, and photography have appeared, or are forthcoming, in journals such as *The Southampton Review, Salamander, RHINO, Alaska Quarterly Review, Pilgrimage, Green Mountains Review, Southwestern American Literature, The Texas Observer,* and *Existere: A Journal of Art & Literature.* His Frontextos (visual poems) have been published in *Poetry Northwest, Texas Review Press, Borderlands: Texas Poetry Review, Midway Journal, The Langdon Review of the Arts in Texas,* and elsewhere. Octavio's visual work has been exhibited in numerous art spaces, including, The Southwest School of Art, Presa House Gallery, Brownsville Museum of Fine Art, and Equinox Gallery. He is the recipient of the Nebrija Creadores Scholarship, consisting of a month-long residency at the Instituto Franklin at Alcalá University in Alcalá de Henares, Spain. He holds a Ph.D. from the University of North Texas and is the regional editor for *Texas Books in Review.* Octavio teaches Literature and Creative Writing in the M.A./M.F.A. program at Our Lady of the Lake University in San Antonio, Texas. Website: octavioquintanilla.com   IG: @writeroctavioquintanilla   Twitter: @OctQuintanilla

Dana Rivera received her film degree from Ithaca College and began her career making documentaries at nonprofit organizations such as the Innocence Project and Legal Services of New Jersey. In her late 20's, she began experimenting with various art forms from water marbling and bookbinding to poetry and digital art, which became her greatest tool for self-exploration and self-expression. Her art is an effort to remember (re-member) her self, through a spectrum of topics from reclaiming the spiritual practices of her latino ancestors to nurturing mental, physical, and emotional health. Dana is currently working on a collection of poetry and abstract art in Washington DC where she resides with her husband and dog.

Joey Salomone was born and raised in the Midwest. Being home schooled, Joey grew up spending much of his time reading and writing. He started writing poetry during his teenage years and continued throughout college and into adulthood. He currently lives and works in Kansas City, MO as a nurse. He continues to read and write poetry daily.

George L. Stein is a photographer with Midwest roots working in the NYC area focused on art and surrealist photographic genres. He has been published recently by Tofu Ink Arts Press, Wrongdoing Magazine and Fatal Flaw. georgelstein.com and on Insta, @steincapitalmgmt.

Myles Weber is a professor of English at Winona State University in Minnesota. His work has appeared in the *Kenyon Review*, the *Southern Review*, the *Georgia Review*, and many other journals. He is the author of *Consuming Silences: How We Read Authors Who Don't Publish* (U of Georgia Press).

Susannah Winters Simpson is a hospice nurse, and she facilitates Therapeutic Writing groups for treatment centers. Her work was accepted by Cream Literary Alliance: Her Voice Series and was read last November at the Norton Museum. Simpson has been published in: *North American Review, Potomac, Wisconsin Review, South Carolina Review, POET, and Nimrod International* among others. Her book *Geography of Love & Exile* was published by Cervena Barva Press *in 2016.* Winters Simpson is a volunteer ESL tutor for DePorres Literacy Center, is the Co-Director of the Performance Poets of the Palm Beaches Reading Series. www.writeRECOVERY.com, write_recovery@IG

Vivien/vonvivsview is a in Vienna based Austrian poetry writer and analog photographer, currently living in New York. As an artist she calls herself "vonvivsview". A couple of months ago she decided to start a blog were she officially releases her poetry together with her analog photography to connect those two together and create a vivid story toeach poetry - even though it's just a captured moment. Currently she releases her poetry only in English. Vivien fell in love with analog photography, because it's the result of the exact moment of reality only on film. No photoshop, no editing. Her own rule is to not take more than 2 pictures form each occasion to make it more special. It is even more exciting to wait if it really turned out the way she saw it through the camera lens after developing the film.

Lily Lavender Wolf is a poet hailing from the Lower East Side of Manhattan. She enjoys long walks exploring nature, the companionship of her gecko, and writing with multi-colored ink while drinking wine. Lily draws inspiration from the world around her: the forest, acoustic music, dive bars, the wonderful world of amative affairs, perfectly ripe fruit. Poetry is her passion, her pastime, her therapy. She will continue to write down her strange thoughts in lyric until her dying breath. Her creative work can be found published in myriad litmags: Wingless Dreamer, MacQueen's Quarterly, From Whispers to

Roars, Metonym Journal, and the Write Launch, to name a few. Feel free to check out her poetry-only Instagram account, @poet.faerie.magic, for more than 800 different pieces from over the years.